Ministering to Your Pastor

Toby Awasum

Treasure House

An Imprint of
Destiny Image® Publishers, Inc.
P.O. Box 310
Shippensburg, PA 17257-0310

"For where your treasure is,
there will your heart be also." Matthew 6:21

ISBN 1-56043-288-8

For Worldwide Distribution
Printed in the U.S.A.

First Printing: 1997   Second Printing: 1998

This book and all other Destiny Image, Revival Press, and Treasure House books are available at Christian bookstores and distributors worldwide.

For a U.S. bookstore nearest you, call **1-800-722-6774**.
For more information on foreign distributors, call **717-532-3040**.
Or reach us on the Internet: **http://www.reapernet.com**

Contents

Dedication

To the Good Shepherd Himself, Jesus Christ,
my Lord and my Savior.
To all the pastors in my life:
Pius Awah, Dan Bencovick, Jim Weathers,
Franklin Lewis, Floyd C. Crouch, Benjamin Williams,
and their loving spouses.
To those pastoring right now or those who have retired,
I heartily dedicate this book to you with love.

Acknowledgments

This book goes out with sincere appreciation for those whose contributions to my life have been significant.

Special gratitude goes to my best friend and loving wife, Jeannette Awasum, and to my three daughters, Mambo, Frui, and Azah, who have sacrificed the most to live with a husband and father who is also a traveling evangelist. I am also indebted to my pastor, Benjamin Williams, and the Spring Road Church for the training and love they have given me over the years. I am grateful also to Rev. Mary Tyler, a beloved mother, for urging me to put this message in book form.

Special thanks go to Keith Carroll, Marsha Blessing, Reggie Powell, and others at Destiny Image Publishers for their contributions, patience, and accommodation of my busy schedule. I also want to acknowledge friends, pastors, and their spouses, known and unknown. My prayers go up for you before our living God. Finally, I give praise and glory to the Chief Shepherd, Jesus Christ my Lord, for the great things He has done.

From the Writer

Brethren in the Lord,

Greetings in His Name.

Ministering to Your Pastor comes to you by way of my wife, Jeannette Awasum, and I from the Lord. Many pastors do not feel comfortable preaching or teaching on this important subject. It is an honored act of God's mercy, therefore, that He has enabled you and my family to come to this revelation so we may be highly privileged to partake of this ministry of supporting our pastors. Many people are not so blessed. Many books have been written addressing pulpit to pulpit or pastor to pastor ministries. However, this is the first I know of that addresses ministering from the pews to the pulpit. Only a few from the pews have actually considered it their duty to minister to the pulpit! If you are not one of that few, we hope you will not only join in but that after prayerfully reading and studying the subject of this book you will become a gospel workers' advocate in your local church and among your Christian brothers and sisters.

However, if you picked this book to search for an academic debate, you have the wrong book in your hands. I am not a writer, nor am I a native English speaker. I am not a pastor, and I have never been one. I am not a scholar, philosopher, or a theologian. If I have any training, it is to be an engineer. But one thing I know, I am called to be an evangelist. I am called to bring the good news of the gospel of Jesus Christ, and by the grace of God what I am presenting on these pages is an aspect of that gospel. The message is the important thing, not the speech or style of writing. If you simply ignore all the worldly clichés and reap the spiritual food from these pages and use that harvest to *minister to your pastor*, then the Holy Ghost will have achieved His goal in giving us the inspiration of this book. To Him should go all the glory and praise.

And when you do minister to your pastor, please be sure that he will "have all, and abound." Then *He will be full* having received of *you* the things which *you* sent. They will be "an odor of a sweet smell, a sacrifice acceptable, well pleasing to God." *And surely, surely, surely, the Lord* "shall supply all your need according to His riches in glory by Christ Jesus. Now unto God and our Father be glory for ever and ever. Amen" (Phil. 4:18-20).

Preface

In the past ten years we have seen too many great men and women of God who are pastors fail in their ministries. Seemingly the enemy is achieving victories where such victories should be almost impossible. But when we look at the current situation carefully, we can obtain an understanding of why such failures have occurred.

Today's pastor is under extreme pressures. He is overworked and sorely underpaid. Today's pastor is expected to be the strong leader in the church, provide the vision for the church, be in charge of the financial aspects of the church, visit the sick, minister to the bereaved, conduct funerals, conduct weddings, counsel even when he is not equipped to do so, be the secretary, prepare the church bulletin, maintain the building and grounds, operate the church bus, and provide entertaining, thought-provoking messages during services. It is expected that not only will he make such sacrifices, but that his entire family will sacrifice welfare, dreams, aspirations, and education for God and the Body of Christ.

As the pastor strives to survive in such a climate, the confidence in ministers is at an all-time low. Since full-time pastors do not go to a standard 9-to-5 job, many if not most of the laity and of course the rest of society believe that pastors have an easy life. They do not realize that the majority of pastors are under extreme stress, that approximately half of the pastors are going through burnout, and more than a third of pastors are ready to quit. What compounds this situation even more is the fact that the majority of pastors do not even have a close friend. They have no intimate friend who will share their hurts, disappointments, concerns, and even joys.[1]

Fortunately, God always provides someone who will stand in the gap—someone who will conduct warfare against principalities, powers, rulers of darkness of this world, and spiritual wickedness in high places on behalf of pastors. The author of *Ministering to Your Pastor*, Tobias Awasum or Toby as we refer to him, is such a man. He has traveled internationally bringing to the laity the ministry of caring for one's pastor. However, he is not able to minister in multiple places at the same time and cannot carry this message everywhere it needs to go. This book sends forth the message of ministering to one's pastor to places where Brother Toby will not be able to go.

Ministering to Your Pastor is inspired of God to fulfill a real need in the Body of Christ today. The author, who is not a pastor, presents this ministry not from a point of self-interest, but from a point of love and care for one's fellow man—the pastor. The author is a man whose eyes have been enlightened by God to the needs of pastors and who truly

---

1. This profile of pastors is provided by the Pastor to Pastor Ministry of Focus on the Family.

practices what he preaches. As you read the book, may God inspire you to give your pastor *double honor* in ways that you have never done before.

Albert I. Chatmon, pastor
Fort Washington, Maryland

Introduction

The year was 1986. We had a new pastor—a yuppie painted with heavy strokes of good deeds and reputation: evangelistic, honorable, upbeat, caring, loving, unselfish, a man of the people. He became an instant mentor to us the youth. Regrettably, we took a lot of his presence for granted and three years later, we begged to redeem the time but it was already too late. Yes, late that summer, a windstorm, the size of Hurricane Hugo, leveled our lives into bits and pieces—the pastor died! Like an early morning dew, he took off, instantly, without warning, absent from the body, to be present with the Lord. He was 35 years old, married with children.

Unlike his coming, he died poor and depleted. Prior to his coming, he practiced law, owned his own home, had his own cars, and a Ph.D. But he left all behind him, moved and took up residence in our state to pastor our church. By the middle of his third year, he had exhausted all his savings, lost the new home he bought, and could barely support his family. Crowning his dilemma came a sudden heart attack that left behind two very tender children, and a widow, penniless, homeless, desperate, and debilitated.

Ironically, he also left us (the church) financially healthy and like many other churches today, we had substantial reserves tucked away in the bank. And at the same time that our church was busy stuffing its bank account, we were like a pit viper, shedding away every skin of responsibility to the pastor's plight; oh yes, he lost his home on our mechanical smiles and silence; with few Amens, he begged in humor for us to give him his flowers while he could smell them. His troubles escalated into his deathbed and beyond for the rest of his family. However, these dilemmas only invoked marked indifference in our hearts. He was finally laid to rest predictably with arrays of bouquets of flowers at which time he could not smell them! Desperate after his death, the widow moved back into her parents' home hundreds of miles away receiving little or no support from "her church family" for her despairing family. It will be fair, and commendable to say that the new pastor, as soon as he came in, took immediate steps to initiate some kind of temporary subsidy for the widow even though she had moved away.

Anyway, convicted and appalled by my mentor's predicament, I came away from his death determined before God Almighty to do all in my power to make the life of my next pastor(s) better than the life of the one I just lost. Questions flooded my mind. I began my quest on what the Bible says about my responsibility toward my pastor. Having encountered a mountain of responsibility that I owed my pastor, I became resolved (by the grace of God) to fend off the forces that are plaguing, frustrating, and forcing the exodus of ministers from the church. This book is a culmination of this quest to minister to my pastor. By the proclamation of this message I pray to the Lord for the spoiling of principalities and powers and the traditions of man that lay in wait in our churches to taunt the pastors. I pray that the church receives this message as a death warrant and puts under our feet the enemies of God's anointed pulpits. In it you will find elements of teachings encouraging the church to create a conducive environment for pastors to get back to giving *themselves continually to prayer, and the ministry of the Word* (see Acts 6:4), and to have opportunities to minister to their own families. Through this message, the Church will be provoked unto good works and strongholds, and the evil imaginations of the intents of the hearts that are set against the pastors will have to bow to the Word—to doctrine, rebuke, correction, reproof, and to instructions unto righteousness.

All over the globe, hundreds of thousands of pastors, missionaries, evangelists, teachers, and their families are facing similar or worse situations. We have often wondered why ministers of the gospel are being "made as the filth of the world, and are the offscouring of all things" (1 Cor. 4:13). This is spiritual warfare; the devil and his angels have transformed into angels of light in our churches and are daring to defy the armies of the living God. The local pastor is the leading candidate on the devil's hit list in the community. And the devil's bounty hunters are sitting on our very own church pews, finance appropriation committees, and other boardrooms, launching fiery darts to undermine the pastor's authority and his welfare.

And why is the pastor such an envied target? Because it is through the preacher that faith enters the heart of one in need of salvation—salvation from sin, sicknesses, principalities, powers, and salvation from the rulers of darkness of this world. There is no doubt, therefore, why the devil is fighting to eliminate the preacher.

> *For with the heart man believeth unto righteousness; and with the mouth confession is made unto salvation. ... For whosoever shall call upon the name of the Lord shall be saved. How then shall they call on Him in whom they have not believed? and how shall they believe in Him of whom they have not heard? and how shall they hear without a preacher? And how shall they preach, except they be sent? as it is written, How beautiful are the feet of them that preach the gospel of peace, and bring glad tidings of good things!*
>
> Romans 10:10,13-15

Sender⇒preacher preaches⇒the one in need hears⇒believes⇒and calls on the Name and is saved!

Yes, there is a chronological chain of events leading up to salvation. The pastor/preacher is a vital link in this chain. He's so vital that the Lord gave a commendation on the preacher—"As it is written, how beautiful are the feet of them that preach the gospel of peace, and bring glad tidings of good things" (v. 15). On the other hand, the devil is sweating his spirits hard trying to sabotage this crucial link by foiling pastors' efforts and maintaining an unbearable environment for them in each church, in the home, and in this world. The pastor as a prime target of satan is barraged at every opportunity by his forces in an attempt to knock him off balance and from the chain. There are already too many soldiers wounded by the sniper fire of the devil's bounty

hunters. We the Church of the living God need to put on the whole armor of God. We need to release our spiritual arsenals in order to unleash the devil off those on the front line and allow our pastors the time they need to fight or continually attend to prayers and the ministry of the Word. The gates of hell shall come crashing down.

Our investigation on the plight of pastors have the Word pointing back to local churches for solutions. Traditionally the pastor has been prone to seeking for *treatment* (not *cure*) for these problems from other pastors, pastors' conferences, counseling, or an outright abandonment of the ministry. Pastors' conferences have their place but their place cannot and shall never take away *your* place designed by God to minister, support, and edify your pastor. In addressing pastors' problems, the solution from outside the local church is only partial and minimal. The Word of God looks at the church as a living body with many members each working together for the edification of one another. The degree of the pastor's effectiveness in doing his duty as pastor to minister to the church depends on the degree of the members doing their duty effectively as members to minister to the pastor. The Word testifies that in the body,

> *But now hath God set the members every one of them in the body, as it hath pleased Him. ... That there should be no schism in the body; but that the members should have the same care one for another. And whether one member suffer, all the members suffer with it; or one member be honoured, all the members rejoice with it. Now ye are the body of Christ, and members in particular.*
>
> 1 Corinthians 12:18,25-27

In order to minister to the pastor or any other member of the local church, the bulk of the responsibility lies within the local body. As long as they are in one body, when the pastor (a member) is not given his due care, other members of the body will suffer. The health of the church is self-evident in this one truth, *that the members should have the same care one for the other.* Even if an infected eye in a body receives the consultation of the best optician, undergoes the world's expert surgery, and receives the best eye salve for its treatment (helps outside the body), it will still take the cooperative working together of the veins, the nerves, the arteries, the muscles, the kidneys, and the entire body to effectively achieve the healing of that eye. In the same way the solution to pastors' many troubles and the key to their spiritual competence in warfare lies in the hands of a holy, praying, loving, serving, supporting obedient membership. Outside help is not a permanent solution; it is temporary; it is the *treatment* and not the *cure.* The members' faithful practice of their duty as Christians is the only prescription and *cure* for the diagnosed problems facing thousands of pastors in our churches.

When the heart refuses to function, the body goes into a shock—a heart attack. When you refuse to do your duty in the church as a member, when you refuse to support your pastor, you endanger the Body of Christ because your actions create bottlenecks (spiritual blood clots) which are seeds of a heart attack—a dead church. And to undertake the Great Commission and turn to His harvest, the last thing the church needs is blood clots. And the last thing the Lord needs is a dead church! *Ministering to Your Pastor* will help

Chapter One

A Day of Trouble for Pastors

...Ye are honourable, but we are despised. Even unto this present hour we both hunger, and thirst, and are naked, and are buffeted, and have no certain dwellingplace.

1 Corinthians 4:10-11

For a majority of pastors in the Body of Christ this is a day of trouble. They have given all they have into the ministry and to their flocks, yet they are now weary and depleted with no relief in sight. Many are uncertain how they can continue in the area of ministry to which God has called them. "This day is a *day of trouble*, and of rebuke, and of blasphemy: for the children are come to the birth, and *there is not strength to bring forth*" (Is. 37:3b). To these pastors, hardship has been a faithful visitor. They are in need of refreshing and ministry to their needs, for otherwise, the Word may not be able to continue to go forth.

Because the people of their churches have failed to see and minister to their need, I meet pastors who are forced to live on welfare and other subsidies. Some testify that they have gone to pick up their promised paycheck, and in its place received shopping bags of green beans, ears of corn, turnips, tomatoes, and heads of cabbage. I doubt many of us would respond favorably if our secular employers treated us in this manner. Nor do I know of any utility company that will accept produce as payment for its services.

Very few pastors actually live in or own their own homes. Many have rented homes all their lives only to leave their families homeless at their death. The purchase of a medical insurance plan is only wishful thinking for hundreds of thousands of pastors. Tuition and fees are increasing in schools, but the meager income salaries of many pastors cannot permit them to send their children to colleges or universities, and in most cases the church membership does not think they have any responsibility in the matter. Despite the example of the early apostles who tried to shed every bit of responsibility that would have interfered with their purpose of ministering the Word and being given to prayer, most churches today force their pastors to carry an overwhelming excess of baggage upon their already overburdened shoulders. As a result, pastors are hanging onto second jobs just to provide food for their families. Others are outright abandoning the ministry and taking on secular jobs.

Most church members pay their taxes and bills faithfully, but very few respect God enough to pay their church dues, give respectable offerings, or be used of Him to feed a hungry "prophet." "Ye have robbed Me in tithes and offerings," God has complained (see Mal. 3:8). Therefore the very people called to minister to the people of God are forced to cling to the lowest rungs of income ladder. This is in addition to

2

you create a blood clot free environment for your local church.

Among other things, you will discover to your amazement, why the laborers are few, and that there is such a thing as ministering from the pews. You'll pick up a unique thought on *giving* and how it is the main agent by God's design for the propagation of the gospel, and for ministering to your pastor. Finally, you are urged to give to your pastor his flowers while he can smell them and you are also given tips on how to do so. This knowledge, if acted upon, provides the believer the opportunity to partake of the Great Commission.

Even though this book articulates ministering, supporting, and encouraging your pastor, and even though the book may be cheered and welcomed by pastors, pastors are not the final beneficiaries of the teaching—you are. If you are failing in your duty and your pastor is running behind as a result, all that is happening in your local church may be mere *intellectual exercises* wedded with good human programming but bearing no spiritual significance to the soul. But if you revere the Word of God, and then minister and encourage your pastor in his duty, you will be the real beneficiary. The best kept secret revealed by this teaching is its astounding "Benefits and Rewards." Observe that he that receives a prophet in the name of a prophet shall receive a prophet's reward (see Mt. 10:41). What a reward! Receiving a preacher's reward without being a preacher! "Nevertheless, when the Son of man cometh, shall He find faith on the earth?" (Lk. 18:8)

What People Are Saying...

I have been in the Church for 46 years and I have never, never heard or seen this truth presented like this—like it is.

Pastor Bynum
Oxon Hill, MD

This is the best message I have ever heard in my life, and I mean every word of it.

Pastor Van Sullivan
Lancaster, SC

I am afraid to say "amen" to every word this brother is saying; someone might think I sat down and discussed the church with him.

Pastor Lanval Hendricks
Queens, NY

So true! This brother challenged me so much with the Word of God that I want to have a pastor of my own to minister to.

Pastor Peters
Orlando, FL

Thank you! Every child of God needs a copy of this book in his or her heart.

Mary Tyler, pastor's wife
Mt. Rainier, MD

We need this teaching in the Church today more than ever before. Don't miss this for anything. This is meat for your soul!

Pastor Joseph Machogu
Suna-Migori, Kenya

the stress they experience from being dependent upon the local church which is one of the most unreliable and unpredictable sources of income and employment. Yet the Church as a Body continues to turn a blind eye and a deaf ear toward these problems!

The majority of pastors must act as if they are walking on egg shells as they carry out their pastoral duties. Not one can afford to "break" a member. Each constantly wonders who will misunderstand him in his next step of performing his duty as a shepherd. In fact, the general trend in most churches is to have the flock shepherding the shepherd and telling him or her what to do. If the pastor doesn't agree he is told to "find another church to 'pastor' "! The membership is prone to expect special consideration at every turn, and some individuals feel that they are doing the pastor and his spouse a favor just by coming to church, paying tithes, giving offerings, reading Scriptures in church, and *praying*! May God have mercy on us!

This undue burden and lack of support has caused many pastors and their spouses to spend many sleepless nights wondering about their calling. Out of frustration and lack of church support many pastors have unfairly questioned their own legitimate calling into the ministry. Our unwitting behaviors as church members are often responsible for the depression, anger, bulimia, and other physical and mental traumas that are experienced by our pastors and their spouses. Some of us feel unwilling to shoulder our responsibility for these situations; we feel that once the pastor has been paid the church doesn't owe him anything else. We do our best to place a cap, or ceiling, on the pastor's blessings. But the Lord who loves a cheerful giver will agree that any form of salary given our pastors should form the *beginning* of our support of our pastors, not the end. If you have a problem with this concept, I challenge you to go before the Lord with it because God's blessings to His people are never capped; they are always overflowing if we allow Him to work and move through us.

In the first century, the apostle Paul said, "Even unto this present hour we both hunger, and thirst, and are naked, and are buffeted, and have no certain dwellingplace" (1 Cor. 4:11). There is no new thing under the sun, is there (see Eccl. 1:9)? Preachers in all ages have been given the short end of the stick. Yet we as the Body of Christ have come into Zion week after week singing the songs of Zion, praying to the God of Zion, and then we leave Zion with no meat for sacrifice or a dwelling place for the servant of God. We enter the gates of God's house with thanksgiving and praise in our hearts, and we have nerve to sit at ease and dine. But when we leave Zion behind, she is left desolate, laid waste, and her priest is abandoned and left to seek after his own welfare.

Do ye not know that they which minister about holy things live of the things of the temple? and they which wait at the altar are partakers with the altar?
1 Corinthians 9:13

What has happened to the share that is to be God's, to the share that He has asked to be left at the altar for the care of His ministry and His ministers? What has happened to the first-fruits God has promised to those who serve before His altar?

4

All the best of the oil, and all the best of the wine, and of the wheat, the firstfruits of them which they shall offer unto the Lord, them have I given thee. And whatsoever is first ripe in the land, which they shall bring unto the Lord, shall be thine; and every one that is clean in thine house shall eat of it.

Numbers 18:12-13

Perhaps these words of Christ more accurately describe the state of our hearts before God when it comes to taking responsibility for the welfare of our pastors and their families:

This people draweth nigh unto Me with their mouth, and honoureth Me with their lips; but their heart is far from Me.

Matthew 15:8

Statistics reveal that a frightening number of pastors are faced daily with the choice of whether to stay or to leave the ministry. Are you aware that your pastor may be struggling with whether to remain in the ministry? Did you know that your pastor may be on welfare or other subsidies? Did you know that your pastor may be completely without any medical insurance right now because of its expense? Do you know if your pastor owns his own home or if he can even afford his monthly rent or mortgage payment? Did you know it is highly likely that your pastor's car or house may be on the verge of repossession (if they have not been already)? Do you care? Did you know that your pastor plans all his activities, including family vacations (if you allow him one), around your own church schedule? Do you really care for him like he does for you?

5

The root cause of most pastors' struggle to remain in the ministry can be traced back to the failure of the local church to provide appropriate support to those pastors. In many ways, pastors have become an *endangered specie*. Many of those who remain are not well enough situated to perform their ministerial duties to acceptable levels before the living God; and we have ourselves, the church membership, to blame. Your pastor is very likely one of those pastors struggling somewhere in-between. Why don't you find out and do something today!

Have you ever wondered how far *your* monthly contributions in church (including tithes and offerings for missions and the poor—the sum total of all your church contributions) might go to meet your pastor's basic needs for transportation, telephone, clothing, or possible emergencies? Also consider the rising costs of education for children, medical expenses, and the infinite number of demands your pastor may have upon his limited resources. Call your pastor today, and if he is forthright with you, you will be overwhelmed by his list of needs. Better still, call your pastor's spouse, and if she is not bashful you will be reaching for your checkbook before you know it.

The church membership is serving as an unknowing accomplice in pushing the gates of hell against the Church of the living God by binding the hands of God's ministers with poverty and deprivation. What kind of members are we in the Lord's Body if we can sit at ease in Zion and not feel the hurt of our own pastors who are dying in need? How can we claim to be the Body of Christ when the pastor, one of the members of the Lord's Body, is suffering, yet we are doing nothing? We have ignored countless opportunities to support and minister to our pastors and their families as we ought. Yes, we have been accomplices to the devil's plots against the Lord's Church. The devil is raging in every local church through many of us who are members, and it is his aim to eliminate the pastor and those whom the Lord has called to minister the Word and be in prayer on behalf of those to whom they minister.

How far we have departed from the Word of the living God! Our lives today in the service of the Lord and His Body is a far cry from the lives and services of the early Church. Many self-professing "believers" who fill the pews and the pulpit week after week live in an illusion of being in the service of the Lord and of being on their way to Heaven. These individuals have never fully considered the tragedy of Ananias and Sapphira (see Acts 5:1-11), but have permitted that same spirit of deception, selfishness, and greed to prevail in the Church today. Many stand convicted today because they have lied to God about "the price of the land."

The Book of Acts testifies that "...the multitude of them that believed were of one heart and of one soul" (Acts 4:32a). But today, even Christians from the same household can barely find common ground on which to agree and work for the common good of the Body. We are missing a vital ingredient, the one that enabled the thousands of persons in the early Church to have one heart and one soul, and this is the very reason why the Church is facing many problems today. Everyone enters the house of God with his own heart and with his own soul (his own little agenda), and the pastor is forced to walk carefully as he executes his pastoral tasks lest he should accidentally obstruct someone's private agenda.

In the early Church, the Body was the priority and the focus of all. In this generation, western individualism has crept in and each person has made himself (or herself) his own priority and focus. This dangerous mentality has even crept into Third World churches. The early church was of one heart and one soul in destiny, in sharing what each one had, in prayer, in the urgency for the work, and in the ministry of the Word.

And the multitude of them that believed were of one heart and of one soul: neither said any of them that ought of the things which he possessed was his own; but they had all things common. And with great power gave the apostles witness of the resurrection of the Lord Jesus: and great grace was upon them all.

Acts 4:32-33

It is only in a body that shares the same heart and soul in which when one member suffers that the others will suffer with it or when one member is honored that all will rejoice (see 1 Cor. 12:26). This gospel was manifested in the early Church, for Acts clearly states:

Neither was there any among them that lacked: for as many as were possessors of lands or houses sold them, and brought the prices of the things that were sold, and laid them down at the apostles' feet: and distribution was made unto every man according as he had need.

Acts 4:34-35

Today, we profess to be Christians, but everyone is busy building an empire for himself. Nobody cares whether the

8

Lord's temple is built or not. We claim that it is "not yet time" to build the Lord's house. Around Christmas and Thanksgiving, we make little fruit baskets for the poor, but the other 363 days a year, we don't care whether the poor eat or not. With the same spirit, we also don't care whether they receive the Lord or not, for if we really cared, we would be working hand-in-hand with our pastors, devoting our prayers and our resources to ensure that the pastor is adequately supported for his calling to win souls. In these last days our efforts to win souls would hardly be enough to exhaust a butterfly!

Have you ever heard your pastor announce that he needed a tooth pulled but did not have the money to go to the dentist? Have you ever heard anything similar? Your pastor or his family may not only need money to have a tooth pulled, but they may also be without any money in spite of the new baby that is due next. Your pastor may be unable to feed his family this very day. His phone may be about to be turned off. Can you imagine your pastor making any one of these announcements? The closest I have heard a pastor say, after much agony, is, "Give me my flowers while I can smell them. Don't wait until I die and then bring me a truckload." (And this particular pastor had his house repossessed and he died too!)

Any pastor who dares to make such a request or allows a genuine need to be known risks falling into a barrage of criticism. He risks the wrath of church members who will call him "ungrateful," "greedy," or a "money lover," even though these titles could not be further from the truth. Even while cautious of this very point, the apostle Paul still felt the charges leveled against him by the Corinthian saints. Wounded, Paul got up saying, "Wait a minute, 'in all things I have kept myself from being burdensome unto you, and so will I keep myself' " (2 Cor. 11:9b).

For the most part, pastors are shy to come to you and me with their needs. Supporting your pastor, or ministering to your pastor, shall never be and has never been a popular subject for any pastor to preach or teach on. Most pastors feel like Paul when it comes to this particular subject. And this feeling is typical of any dedicated pastor who wants you for the heavenly Father and not your possessions. These pastors will say with Paul, "I am [become] all things to all men, that I might by all means save some" (1 Cor. 9:22b). For this reason, pastors' spouses will agree with me that most pastors go to their graves with truckloads of problems that the church should have known but did not. Some do not want to hurt our feelings, and others fear that the church would respond in a less-than-friendly fashion.

Today, a spirit of *cowardice* exists in pastors in regard to teaching on *supporting your pastor*. This in my opinion is not healthy for a sincere child of God who is seeking to please God in every area of his or her life. This lack of courage to teach the truth of God's Word breeds sin, ignorance, and eventual destruction of the body and soul of the child of God. A man of knowledge increases strength (see Prov. 24:5), and it is the knowledge of the truth that makes us free (see Jn. 8:32). How can we be made free if the truth is kept from us? Let's embrace and teach this truth without compromise. It is the duty of man to obey God and keep His commandments. The Lord is still saying to the pastors, teachers, and evangelists what He said to Jeremiah:

*...Gird up thy loins, and arise, and speak unto them **all** that I command thee: be not dismayed at their faces, lest I confound thee before them.*

Jeremiah 1:17

Like Paul with the Corinthian church, pastors have undergone scrutiny, cross examination, and even challenge to their office as pastor and as persons who deserve our care. Pastors are constantly and passively on the defensive as to what the church membership may say, feel, think, and do concerning their welfare. In spite of this, "the gifts and calling of God are without repentance" (Rom. 11:29)! God's words regarding ministering to a man of God are still as valid today as they ever were; and the Spirit of the Lord moved on Paul to instruct Timothy, saying,

Let the elders that rule well be counted worthy of double honour, especially they who labour in the word and doctrine. For the scripture saith, Thou shalt not muzzle the ox that treadeth out the corn. And, The labourer is worthy of his reward.

1 Timothy 5:17-18

From this and other Scriptures, it seems pretty clear to me that in the eyes of the Almighty God, taking care of the pastor is a paramount duty of the local church. If a doctor naturally eats of the fruits of his labor, if a lawyer naturally eats of the fruits of his labor, if a farmer naturally enjoys the fruits of his labor, why does your pastor have to defend his right? The workman is still worthy of his hire. We have a duty; it is to fear God and keep His commandments (see Eccl. 12:13). The Lord has said, "Let him that is taught in the word communicate unto him that teacheth in all good things" (Gal. 6:6). We need to stand up to this truth instead of forcing our pastors into a state of paranoia.

Be open to hearing the Word of the Lord on this issue. There are clear scriptural principles that address the necessity of our giving and of caring for those whom God has called to be the shepherds of His flock. For too long our pastors have suffered lack and deprivation because of our ignorance, and even our direct disobedience to biblical truth. Don't wait until it is too late to open your heart and your resources to your minister. Are you restraining the advance of God's Kingdom by your failure to properly care for the pastor God has placed over you? Will yet another valuable laborer be forced out of the work of the harvest because you failed to see his need and the needs of his family?

Chapter Two

"The Labourers Are Few..."

And Jesus went about all the cities and villages, teaching in their synagogues, and preaching the gospel of the kingdom, and healing every sickness and every disease among the people. But when He saw the multitudes, He was moved with compassion on them, because they fainted, and were scattered abroad, as sheep having no shepherd. Then saith He unto His disciples, The harvest truly is plenteous, but the labourers are few; pray ye therefore the Lord of the harvest, that He will send forth labourers into His harvest.

Matthew 9:35-38

The Lord of the harvest has declared the *magnitude* of the harvest. The harvest is plenteous, and that it is great. He has also declared the *urgency* of the harvest by warning against complacency.

Say not ye, There are yet four months, and then cometh harvest? behold, I say unto you, Lift up your eyes, and look on the fields; for they are white already to harvest.

John 4:35

13

With *time* and *magnitude* as the main constrains in accomplishing the task, basic laws of economics demand a *large labor force* to finish the harvest in the limited time available to us. But something strange is happening when it comes to the economics of the gospel ministry. Here, we find a vast shortage of labor in spite of the great magnitude of the harvest. In fact, if the great multitude of sheep "scattered abroad" were all to be assigned shepherds, the gospel ministry would potentially rate as the number one employing occupation in the world. But what do the actual facts reveal? *The laborers are few.* In spite of the great need, there is no corresponding plenteousness in the labor force!

Why is this the case? Does it have something to do with church management or church people? What is it about this job that causes the basic laws of supply and demand to break down? Why do the economics of the ministry appear to follow a different set of rules than practically every other field affected by supply and demand? Why? The answer; there are wolves in the sheepfold. There are bugs in the system. There are moles and weeds in the church harvestfield.

The Epistle of Jude speaks of "certain men [who] crept in unawares" (see Jude 4). These men are those who instead of working for the system, actually work against it. They have little regard for the unsaved multitude. They care more about preserving the church's money than "spending and being spent" for the salvation of souls. Therefore it is noteworthy that the Lord of the harvest says to His disciples, "...The harvest truly is great, but the labourers are few: pray ye therefore the Lord of the harvest, that He would send forth labourers into His harvest. Go your ways: behold, I send you forth *as lambs among wolves*" (Lk. 10:2-3).

14

These are the ones that are cooking it day and night to run the pastor out, to frustrate the pastor, and to be the pastor's employer. Where do you stand? Are you working for the system or against it? Do you pay your church dues faithfully or do you only pay them when you like? The latter is the act of a wolf in sheep's clothing and frustrates the system. The conditions under which the pastors of these wolves must work contribute to pushing these men and women right out of the ministry.

> Some onlookers thought it was unusual, but few noticed when the pastor wheeled into the church parking lot in a borrowed pickup truck. But everyone's eyes were upon him when he backed the truck across the lawn to his study door. Refusing comment or assistance, he began to empty his office onto the truck bed. He was impassive and systematic: first the drawers, then the files, and last his library books, which he tossed carelessly into a heap, many of them flopping askew like slain birds. His task done, the pastor left the church and, as was later learned, drove some miles to the city dump where he committed everything to the waiting garbage. It was his way of putting behind him… This young, gifted pastor was determined never to return to the ministry. Indeed, he never did (Kent and Barbara Hughs, *Liberating Ministry from the Success Syndrome*, Wheaton, IL: Tyndale House Publishers, 1987, p. 9).

Oh Jerusalem, Jerusalem

Why are the laborers few? We are killing and running out the prophets! Let the Word of God speak to you.

Wherefore, behold, I send unto you prophets, and wise men, and scribes: and some of them ye shall kill and crucify; and some of them shall ye scourge in your synagogues, and persecute them from city to city: that upon you may come all the righteous blood shed upon the earth, from the blood of righteous Abel unto the blood of Zacharias son of Barachias, whom ye slew between the temple and the altar. Verily I say unto you, All these things shall come upon this generation. O Jerusalem, Jerusalem, thou that killest the prophets, and stonest them which are sent unto thee, how often would I have gathered thy children together, even as a hen gathereth her chickens under her wings, and ye would not! Behold, your house is left unto you desolate.

Matthew 23:34-38

The blood of all the prophets, apostles, evangelists, pastors, and teachers killed, as well as all the righteous blood that has been shed upon the earth, is on your head today (unless you repent) because of all the ills you are causing God's servants (see Mt. 23:35)! The laborers are few because we have not treated those that we have in the way of the Lord. And we wonder why some of our churches are empty? We have been helping the devil to frustrate the work of the Lord. The laborers are few because we have been on the necks of the laborers like a wolf on a lamb's neck while all the other sheep that have seen it are running for their lives. Let go, in the name of Jesus Christ!

Some of the laborers are running for their lives. Others are running for the lives of their families. Paul addressed the church in Corinth, saying, "...I will not be burdensome to you: for I seek not yours, but you: for the children ought not to lay up for the parents, but the parents for the children. And I will very gladly spend and be spent for you, though the more abundantly I love you, the less I be loved" (2 Cor. 12:14-15). Now Paul did not have a wife or a child. What a burden the church would have claimed if he had!

A Pastor on Welfare

Picture your pastor standing in line for food stamps. It does happen. Many clergy today find it necessary to receive government assistant to feed their families; I am one of them.

I'm a full-time pastor of an upper-middle class church of 300 members in a mainline denomination. I have a B.A. degree in psychology and a master of divinity degree from a major seminary. I've been married twelve years and have two children. I have committed my life to Christ.

Yet the government has to supplement my income by providing food stamps as well as the Earned Income Credit, which comes through my income taxes, and the free lunch program that my daughter receives in the public school.

How can this be? Even though lay people attempt to do all they can to alleviate world suffering, they often allow their pastor to subsist on the lowest level of income possible.

My wife and I were once able to say we earned everything we received. We worked hard and were paid accordingly. In the ministry it's different. I work all available hours as the "pastor in charge." Whether I work forty hours or eighty hours I receive the same salary, even though I might drive twice the number of miles and spend twice as much for expenses. The harder I work, the more unreimbursed expenses I incur.

Maybe you think my wife should work outside the home. But our children are small, and with the strains of parsonage life, we believe they need their mother's presence.

Somehow it all seems wrong. The pastor should be free to serve God and the people who need him without having to fight the depressing battle of staying alive financially. The pastor's children should not have to grow up in such stark contrast to the lifestyles of the children whose church he serves. They should not have to be "second class" citizens.

If those who are lay leaders in the church should give thought to this social problem of the twentieth-century pastor, improvement would be made. The expenses of the ministry are higher than ever and should come out of the church's treasury. The members should sincerely try to determine what their pastor's family needs in the way of financial support. What is your pastor doing without? More importantly what is his family doing without? Are his children growing up with a good impression of the Church's love and care? Will they be able to receive the necessary education to cope in an increasingly technological world?

Is your pastor eligible for welfare?

Anonymous (Reprinted from *Eternity*, September 1980, 65)

Accounts like the one above are not isolated or exceptional incidents. If we claim to be part of the living Body of Christ here on earth, how can the government and/or the parents of pastors be subsidizing pastors' living expenses while other members of the same living Body are basking in luxury, irresponsible and unconcerned?

How many of us in the local church really care about what the pastor and his family are going through? Very few church members actually understand that their pastors are capable of landing other professional jobs that would carry similar, if not better, benefits than are enjoyed by most of their congregations. The church membership often doesn't know or care that their pastor gave up a good job with solid benefits in order to come and pastor them. However, a concerned and educated church member will soon realize that the benefits offered him at his job are not likely available to his pastor through the church. Further study and investigation will reveal that these same benefits are five to ten times more expensive if the pastor has to go out and purchase medical insurance or other necessary benefits as an independent person. Because of the expense, many pastors end up having no medical or health insurance, and when a family member does need medical care, they end up spending even more money when they already don't have enough to cover all their needs!

These deficiencies frighten people from the ministry. Some choose to be part-time ministers, and others are forced completely out of the ministry and back into secular occupations. But with the harvest white and ready with billions of unsaved souls out there in the world, shouldn't the church be *recruiting* laborers? Can she afford to lose any? With the amount of work to be done can we afford to have any minister serving only on a part-time basis? Many today have mentally criticized and condemned the rich young ruler because he could not part from his wealth (see Lk. 18:18-23), yet they have turned around and fallen into the same trap. Many church members claim to have been baptized into the Body of Christ, but they have carefully left their wallets, purses, and other resources out of the water and unbaptized.

The need for ministers to work in the Lord's harvest cannot be understated. The human race is dying in its need of the Bread of Life, Jesus Christ; for "man shall not live by bread alone, but by every word that proceedeth out of the mouth of God" (Mt. 4:4b). No man goes to the Father except by the Word (see Jn. 1:1; 14:6). Without the Word, we can do nothing (see Jn. 15:5), nor can we be saved. The Word is the power of God unto salvation (see Rom. 1:16). And the world needs the Word to be preached to them. The harvest must be gathered in while there is still time.

However, as our world marches more and more into perilous times, this task has become increasingly difficult. The world's population is increasing, and iniquity is at an all-time high. The conditions truly reveal a harvest that is white and ripe. Yet because the love of many is waxing cold and because individualism and greed is spreading within the camp (the Church), support for the laborers is dwindling. As a result, an increasingly greater number of souls are in danger of not partaking of the Bread of Life. Great portions of the harvestfield are left entirely untouched.

Your pastor's duties require him, not only to labor for the salvation of souls, but also to watch over the souls in his charge as one who must given an account (see Heb. 13:17). Observing the importance of the pastor's work, it is no surprise, therefore, that satan is fighting with all his might to eliminate ministers of the Word. Pastors after God's own heart are an endangered species. The devil's efforts have effectively caused many local assemblies to dismiss, despise, frustrate, and render impotent both the pastor and his office. Once again, this has greatly contributed to the exodus of many pastors and evangelists from the ministry.

The Cost of Being a Minister

A pastor is a man well grounded in the Word and knows his responsibility before God to answer his call as well as to provide for his family (see 1 Tim. 5:8). These two responsibilities should not have to be contrary to one another. However, let's look at some statistics and the financial realities of serving the Body of Christ as a pastor. I believe these harsh facts will not only substantiate why there is such a shortage of laborers, but they will cause you to wonder why there are as many laborers as there are.

The following statistics have been drawn from the book *Pastors at Risk* by H.B. London and Neil B. Wiseman (Wheaton, IL: Victor Books, 1993 pp. 114-115, 127, 163). These statistics reveal:

- 33% of pastors surveyed considered leaving the ministry in the last three months.

- 70% of pastors indicated that their compensation contributed to conflict in their marriage.

- 22% feel forced to supplement their church income.

- 73% felt they were underpaid.

- 74% of clergy report experiencing periods of major distress.

- 81% say their marriage problems were a result of insufficient time spent together; 71% say it was as a result of the use of money; and 70% say it was as a result of their *income level*.

Some members of the church feel that they are the pastor's employer. They claim that because *they are paying* him, they can order him or constrain him in any way they want. But the Lord says we are workers together with Him (see 2 Cor. 6:1). This includes the Lord, the pastor, and every member of the church. To the pastor, God says,

Feed the flock of God which is among you, taking the oversight thereof, not by constraint, but willingly; not for filthy lucre, but of a ready mind; neither as being lords over God's heritage, but being ensamples to the flock. And when the chief Shepherd [the owner of both the pastor and the members] *shall appear, ye shall receive a crown of glory that fadeth not away.*

1 Peter 5:2-4

Based on God's clear Word, I have no idea where these church members got the idea that they are the pastor's employer. In seeking for laborers in the gospel, the Lord is not looking for "prophets for hire" like Balaam. God Himself has called and chosen certain persons for the ministry of the Word. Their job is a divine appointment, and so is the pay. Whatever we do *with God* to compensate the pastor, we are doing it to God. Paul addressing the Philippian saints said, "Ye sent once and again unto my necessity. Not because I desire a gift: but I desire fruit that may *abound to your account.* But I have all, and abound: I am full, having received…the things which were sent from you, *an odor of a sweet smell, a sacrifice acceptable, wellpleasing to God* (Phil. 4:16b-18). Therefore, it is not to the pastor but to God that we pay tithes, give offerings, and provide for the needs of the pastor. We know that no amount of pay on earth will ever truly compensate the minister for his work, neither can our reward for supporting pastors be measured in earthly terms.

Needless to say, the demon of salary has often created a roadblock to supporting our pastors. Many brethren look at what we call "pastors' salaries," their eyes bulging with envy claiming that the salaries are supposed to take care of all the pastors' needs. Some members don't even like the idea that their pastors may receive salaries greater than what they may receive at their own jobs. Shame on you if you feel that way! On the other hand, many pastors like Paul seek to preach the gospel free. Pastors who are "hired prophets" will not preach you to Heaven; they will be obligated to preach what their "employers" want to hear, thereby compromising the Word! But those that God has called stay and feed the sheep faithfully, without respect of persons or salaries. Yet God's calling to His servants does not negate our obligation to provide for them in abundance, according to the Word of the Lord.

David said, "My cup runneth over" (Ps 23:5b). The Lord says, "Give, and it shall be given unto you" (Lk. 6:38a). Paul says that God is able to give and to do exceedingly abundantly above what we can ask or even think (see Eph. 3:20). The Father says, "If you give, I will open the windows of heaven such that you will not have room enough to keep what I shall give to you" (see Mal. 3:10). You shall be the head and not the tail (see Deut. 28:13). Eyes have not seen, nor have ears heard all that God has for those who love Him (see 1 Cor. 2:9). It appears to me that in spiritual things, there is always a flowing, or running, over. However our finance committees keep fighting to place a cap on what the Lord wants to fill above the brim!

Therefore if salaries even have to be considered, they should be the *beginning point* of meeting the needs of the pastor and not the end! Salaries should ensure the bear minimum to meet the pastor's needs, but they should not place a limit on his receiving. If we make his salary the final say for his receiving, it appears to me that we are not allowing room for his cup to run over, nor for his good measure to flow over. In a sense, we cut the pastor's blessings short by considering his salary to be the one and final point of meeting his needs every month.

Some persons believe that pastors should work secular jobs to supplement their salaries, and many are doing that to feed their families. Those that hold to this view always cite Paul's tent making. Yet it was out of the hardness of the people's hearts that Paul decided to work to feed himself rather than force the issue or demand his rights for full support from unwilling givers (see 1 Cor. 9:15-23)! This did not mean that Paul sanctioned secular employment for ministers of the gospel. (Chapter Six addresses Paul's actual position in more detail.) We all know that taking on a secular job adds more work, stress, and burnout to the pastor and renders him less effective in the ministry. The same people who hold to the unscriptural perspective that a minister should support himself and his family through secular employment are often the first at the committee table to negotiate down the pastor's salary. However, this message is not addressed to committees, it is to the Church. I want to inform you, my friend, that in spite of those committees you can still make a difference in your pastor's life by ministering to him as a member in the Body of Christ. This is pleasing to God.

Persons often balk over the thought of the pastor's salary, but these same persons have little concept of how short that salary falls of truly meeting the needs of the pastor and his family. The median salary for metropolitan pastors in the United States is $28,000. This amount is not sufficient to even pay tuition for three in a Christian school or one child in the university, let alone buy food for the family, entertain visitors, pay bills (electric, phone, gas, books, heat, etc.), buy a health insurance plan, pay a home mortgage or rent, pay for the car, the auto insurance, or provide for emergencies! And this does not consider or take into account any previous debt the pastor and his wife may have accrued as part of their college or seminary education; education they received for the sole purpose of becoming better equipped to care for you and your fellow church members.

Let's get over the fact that the mathematics of God's economy is not the same as man's. We may hang on to our meager salaries for our pastors and make a big deal out of them, but in the eyes of the living God they are merely the tip of the iceberg. Don't be the one holding back the pastor's blessings on the assumption that you are doing the will of God because your pastor already receives a salary. His salary is only the beginning point of meeting his needs.

I hope you have begun to get a clear picture of the great need there is among our pastors today. Even if your pastor receives a salary, it is not likely that it comes close to meeting the great list of needs in his life. God has called us to pray for additional laborers, yet how can we expect persons to be able to serve God to their full capacity when we fail to equip and support them as we have been called to do. In the mathematics of God's economy we will be blessed if we are willing to bless, and God will call laborers to fill the vast need we see all around us if we are willing to shoulder our own responsibility to support and bless the laborers with which He has blessed us. Can we expect God to continue to call and send His choicest servants while we hinder the work of His Kingdom by refusing to care for the laborers He loves?

Chapter Three

The Work of a Pastor

*For whosoever shall **call** upon the name of the Lord shall be saved. How then shall they call on Him in whom they have not **believed**? and how shall they believe in Him of whom they have not **heard**? and how shall they hear without a **preacher**? And how shall they preach, except they be **sent**? as it is written, How beautiful are the feet of them that preach the gospel of peace, and bring glad tidings of good things! ... So then faith cometh by hearing, and hearing by the word of God.*

Romans 10:13-15,17

We have already seen what our Lord Himself said of the magnitude and urgency of the harvestfield, yet we have also noted that we are responsible for the shortage of laborers due to our unwillingness to adequately care for God's servants so they can fully give themselves to the work to which He has called them. Many pastors have left or are leaving the ministry. Great numbers of those who remain are totally dependent on secular jobs. This is not healthy for the Church of

God. It is not a credit to the Lord, nor is it a good witness for the gospel.

From our passage in Romans, we can clearly see the **chain** of responsibilities involved before a soul steps out in faith to claim the promise of salvation from God Almighty. The Word of God becomes the object of the hearer's faith as he calls to the Lord for redemption. Received with faith, the Word of God forms his thoughts, regulates his actions, and molds his life. The manifestation of the faith gained from the Word is the earnest call of the helpless depraved man to the merciful Lord and Savior. However, this cannot happen unless the Word is first *heard*. The Word cannot be implanted to bring about the necessary change and faith to bring the hearer to salvation unless there is a *preacher* through whom the Word is made known to the hearer: "And how shall they *hear* without a *preacher*?" There must be a preacher to present the spoken Word.

The Word of God is fallen and depraves man's only window of opportunity to escape the eternal consequences for his sin. The Word of God serves as a map to guide him to salvation from his fallen state and from the enemy. However with this opportunity comes faith and power over the enemy. With the knowledge and application of the Word, the hearer will be equipped to pull down strong holds and every work of the enemy that exalts itself against the knowledge of God (see 2 Cor. 10:4-5). Is it any wonder that the enemy is working so hard to eliminate ministers of the Word or to render powerless those who remain in ministry? As members of the Body of Christ it is our duty to do everything in our power to care for the needs of the pastor who must constantly be on

28

the front line of presenting the Word of God to the unsaved and using the Word to edify us as saints and bring us to spiritual maturity (see Eph. 4:11-13). We must equip him to devote himself to the Word and the teaching of the Word without the distraction of worrying about his daily needs or those of his family.

The first apostles understood the necessity of giving themselves continually to prayer and to the ministry of the Word. This is why they instructed the early believers to choose out overseers to take care of the tasks that would distract them from the responsibilities of their calling:

> *Wherefore, brethren, look ye out among you seven men of honest report, full of the Holy Ghost and wisdom, whom we may appoint over this business. But we will give ourselves continually to prayer, and to the ministry of the word.*
>
> Acts 6:3-4

God has a program to redeem the world, and the worst thing we can do is rob our pastor of the time he needs to devote to prayer before the Lord and to the study of the Word. If your pastor is not able to maintain a life of constant study of the Word and prayer to God, all that may be happening in your church and with your pastor in His service may be merely activities of the soul and not God's Spirit. A pastor who does not pray is hazardous to the church of God, for prayer is the only avenue by which he can receive directives from the Lord. If the pastor is not able to dedicate himself to these tasks, he will begin to transmit his own ideology and the church will become a fleshly, rather than a spiritual, entity.

Evangelist Zacharias Tanee Fomum wrote in his book, *The Practice of Intercession*, "the only work for the Lord that will last is a work conceived in prayer, carried out in prayer, and consummated in prayer. All else is wood, hay, stubble and will certainly not be of any benefit to the church and neither will they be of any consequence to the Father" (New York, NY: Vantage Press, Inc., 1991, p. 16). Your pastor's job is a divine appointment that will not be accomplished by might or by power, but the Spirit of God, and only by His Spirit (see Zech. 4:6). Prayer is the only means by which the work of the Lord can be accomplished here on earth, and the Word is a lamp unto our feet and a light for our path to illumine for us the will of the Lord. The Word brings faith and the prayer of faith manifests the will of the Lord, which was ordained before the foundations of the world.

The pastors who do not seek the Lord become brutish. They will not prosper, and all their flocks shall be scattered (see Jer. 10:21). No flesh shall glory in God's presence and neither will the works of the flesh. It is in prayerfully studying the Word that the pastor seeks the face of God and finds out what the Lord wants to say to His people. Much of the lukewarm condition of our churches is due to the fact that our pastors are not talking to and receiving from God. We must allow our ministers the opportunity of spending time before God by ministering and supporting them in such a way that they will not need to spend time fending for themselves; rather they can give themselves to fending for the Church through the labor of prayer and the study of the Word.

If the early saints needed to assist the apostles and appoint persons to lift unnecessary tasks from their shoulders, how much more should this be true for us in these last and perilous days? In the Church, prayer and study of the Word should not be held second to anything, even though there are many other things that may sound worthwhile or important. Your pastor must spend time before God and speak to Him on behalf of those of whom he shall one day give account (see Heb. 13:17).

Many people today still believe that pastorship is for those who could not make any other headway in life—the frustrated and the unsuccessful. They consider pastors to be those who did not have the courage or the ability to study science, engineering, medicine, business, or other professional areas. This point of view has led many persons to disrespect those who are in full-time ministry. And I must admit that this is what I grew up believing about pastors and others who were born again.

When I was nine years old my great-grandmother (a Presbyterian) asked me to become a pastor when I grew up, but I snubbed the whole idea. Why? I was a young, proud Roman Catholic altar boy, and I felt that her idea of a career for me would be "condescending." At that time and age all I knew and respected were the images of the Catholic priests, or "fathers" in their snow white cassocks. The only image that I had of a pastor was one of a poorly-dressed, common-looking man, who made a shabby image compared to the impressive robes of priests! And my own source of wisdom, my great-grandmother actually wanted me to condescend to become one of them! No, it was too big for me to swallow, and I snubbed her for suggesting it. *How wrong I was!*

Twenty-two years have passed and things have changed! Thank God Almighty, I am happy to be born again, and I am devoting my life to the cause of my Lord, Jesus Christ, and His pastors who I once held in such low esteem. As I recall my sweet great-grandmother, she was angelically patient with me, a stupid young boy who thought he knew everything. In retrospect, I must admit that the old African proverb still holds true: "What an old man (or woman) can see sitting down, a young man cannot see standing up."

I have now come to learn from the Lord that pastoring and ministering in the gospel is the single most important calling that anyone on this earth could ever be privileged to serve in. Pastors may hunger and thirst, be without proper clothing, and be buffeted about with no certain dwelling place. They may labor, working with their own hands, while being reviled, persecuted, and suffering. They may be defamed, and made like the filth of the world and "the off-scouring of all things," but God says that these are the most blessed of the children born of a woman (see 1 Cor. 4:10-16; Mt. 11:11). For nobody's feet are as beautiful as the feet of them that preach the gospel of peace, and bring glad tidings of good things (see Rom. 10:15). What a blessing to be called and given as God's gift to His Church for her edification!

As important as this calling may be, pastors climb *down* to the lowest level of the income ladder when they obey their calling. Yet this is the only "job" so honored by the Lord Jesus Himself that He admonished us to pray for additional persons to be added to the workforce (see Mt. 9:38). It is the only single job that any man or woman, whether they be an engineer, physician, musician, artist, or professor, could trade his or her professions for and never live to regret it. Praise be to God!

...For we are made a spectacle unto the world, and to angels, and to men. We are fools for Christ's sake, but ye are wise in Christ; we are weak, but ye are strong; ye are honourable, but we are despised. Even unto this present hour we both hunger, and thirst, and are naked, and are buffeted, and have no certain dwell-ingplace; and labour, working with our own hands: being reviled, we bless; being persecuted, we suffer it: being defamed, we entreat: we are made as the filth of the world, and are the offscouring of all things unto this day.

1 Corinthians 4:9-13

The language of First Corinthians 4:9-13 brings to mind an image of the minister as a doomed gladiator being dragged to the arena. The minister is "set forth" by God as a doomed gladiator to serve the world at all costs. However, many believers never realize that the screaming angry mob in the arena of the Roman empire has been replaced today by church members themselves. The Lord's warning to His followers, "Behold, I send you forth as sheep in the midst of wolves: be ye therefore wise as serpents, and harmless as doves" (Mt. 10:16), is always viewed from the perspective that the wolves Jesus spoke of are the non-believers. However, if you look carefully, you will see that there are wolves sitting in the front pews of your church. Satan has truly transformed himself into an angel of light (see 2 Cor. 11:14)!

Pastors have been "appointed to death" (1 Cor. 4:9). The Preacher's Online Study Bible (Chattanooga, TN: Leadership Minstries Worldwide, 1992, Vol. 8, p. 70) points out that ministers in the early Church were frequently dragged through the city streets and then thrown before the screaming mobs of the arena. They were made a spectacle before the world, and they endured it for the cause of Christ. Even when most believers manage to avoid persecution, pastors are still considered fools for Christ's sake. Pastors are often without honor among the world, and sadly, they are often without honor or respect among believers too. No one walks around with a sign declaring that there is no honor in pastoring like there is in practicing medicine or engineering, but it is still manifested in the rejection, ridicule, and persecution experienced by pastors and other ministers of the gospel.

True ministers have the mind of Christ that comes with the rejection and persecution. Like Jesus, they are willing to pay any price to share the gospel and minister to people in need. Paul said that he and the other apostles were bearing these very sufferings "even unto this present hour" (1 Cor. 4:11). Pastors are still bearing these very sufferings "even unto this present hour," and sadly enough, much of it is at the hands of believers. Their lack of food and clothing is nothing new. Being clubbed, buffeted, pushed about, slapped, and imprisoned is common occurrence. Having no certain dwelling place is nothing new to most pastors, even though this might surprise many believers. Using money earned from a secular job to run the church and preach the gospel is a normal practice for many pastors and evangelists today. At every turn, ministers have turned the other cheek when defamed and made the filth and the scum of the world.

Many of us subscribe to being part of the Body of Christ, but we are doing nothing to keep the Body healthy. We have done nothing but revile the Body. Very few of us are actually suffering to have the gospel preached to our world that is dying without Christ. Few believers have actually given their all for Christ's sake and for the gospel's sake. "A man's life consisteth not in the abundance of the things which he possesseth" (Lk. 12:15b), but we still have more cars than garages, more clothes than closet space, and the gospel is going out at the expense of the obedient few. I have been to places where I have literally taken off and given away my suit, tie, and socks, and preached in a T-shirt because of what I saw the pastors putting on! How much are we throwing away or sacrificing to meaningless things that could be useful to the pastors out in the fields that are ripe and white and ready for harvest?

Is this the value that we place on the Word of God and those who minister it to us? Is our estimated worth of the very Word that brings us faith and salvation adequate? Perhaps we are more guilty of loving the world than the *Word*. Yet it is in the Word and on the promises found in the Word that our very hope is based. We need to value God's Word. We need to immerse ourselves in its life-giving message. We need to abide by it and let it be made flesh in us. And we need to demonstrate our obedience and love for God through ministering to those called by God to minister His Word. If we are honest, we will each be forced to admit that not one of us would be children of God today if someone somewhere down the line had not responded to God's call to minister the gospel. And without the life-giving Word we have been taught through God's pastors, how many of us would have had the strength or the knowledge to move on and begin to mature in the Lord? We all would have lost our hope and power a long time ago.

Jesus knows that in moments of desperation man often loses track of the salvation power of the living Word in the Scriptures. This is why throughout the Bible He admonishes us to trust in the Word. To Joshua He commanded, "This book of the law shall not depart out of thy mouth; but thou shalt meditate therein day and night, that thou mayest observe to do according to all that is written therein: for then thou shalt make thy way prosperous, and then thou shalt have good success" (Josh. 1:8). In Proverbs 3:4-5, He commands, "Trust in the Lord [the Word] with all your heart and do not lean unto your own understanding but in everything acknowledge Him and He will direct your path." In Psalm 1 He says the man who delights in the law of the Lord and meditates on it day and night shall be like a tree planted by the rivers of water and that whatever he does will prosper.

Another Psalm teaches us that the Word of God is a lamp unto our feet and a light to our paths (see Ps. 119:105). What we often find in the pages of Scriptures often sounds good, but we find it difficult to translate into action and actual benefit. However it should not be like that. After every session of hearing from the Lord through meditation, preaching, and/or the study of the Word, we should be able to come away *revived*. The importance of this fact is underlined by the seriousness with which the Lord addresses John the Baptist's despair when he demanded to know from prison, "Art thou He that should come, or do we look for another?" (Mt. 11:3)

This is the same John who when he saw the Lord coming in the Jordan valley declared, "Behold the Lamb of God, which taketh away the sin of the world. This is He of whom

I said, After me cometh a man which is preferred before me: for He was before me" (Jn. 1:29b-30). This is the same John who witnessed the Spirit descending from Heaven like a dove upon Jesus (see Mt. 3:16). This same prophet testified that Jesus was indeed the Son of God and also witnessed that Jesus must increase and he must decrease (see Jn. 3:28-30). But when this same man of God was faced with persecution from Herod he did as we all do at times; he wondered and demanded to know from the Lord, "Art thou He that should come, or do we look for another?" How many times have we cried out, "Lord, where are You?"

Jesus could have disappeared from where He was teaching and reappeared in John the Baptist's prison cell to comfort and reassure him that He was indeed the one. But the Lord did not do that. He chose to *preach* the Word of God to John. By this He was saying, "Don't look at the circumstances but instead look at the Word." To emphasize this point of depending on the living Word of the Scriptures, He began to preach on Isaiah 29 and 35:

> *...Go and shew John again those things which ye do hear and see: the blind receive their sight, and the lame walk, the lepers are cleansed, and the deaf hear, the dead are raised up, and the poor have the gospel preached to them.*
>
> Matthew 11:4-5

After responding to John the Baptist's question, Jesus went on to open our vision to the greatness of one born of a woman who enters the Kingdom of Heaven (see Mt. 11:11-12). He knew you and I would not have Him, the Word made flesh, living with us in bodily form. Jesus knew we would have to depend on the preaching of the Word to revive and nourish our spirits. Jesus had only 33 years to be here on earth, but His life was a manifestation of the Word of God that would live for all ages to come. Jesus had to remind John the Baptist (and Christians in all ages to come) to depend on the written Word and not on His physical body presence.

We know how the prophets who by the hearing of God's Word received faith through which they "subdued kingdoms, wrought righteousness, obtained promises, stopped the mouths of lions, quenched the violence of fire, escaped the edge of the sword, out of weakness were made strong, waxed valiant in fight, turned to flight the armies of the aliens" (Heb. 11:33-34). The Lord did not want us to lose this and begin to wait around for apparitions. It was by the *preaching* of the Word that Nineveh, the Jews in Egypt, the multitude at Pentecost, and many others recorded in the Word received faith and salvation. As it is written, faith comes by hearing, and hearing by the Word of God (see Rom. 10:17). What a mighty calling it is to be a minister of the Word, to be a pastor called to reap a harvest of souls, to preach the Word to God's people and thereby equip them with the faith to walk in the purposes of God! What an awesome responsibility!

Jesus Christ the Model Preacher:

Another example of the reviving power of ministry of the Word is vividly illustrated by the Lord Jesus Himself as He ministered the need to two of His disciples at a time of great discouragement. I first encountered this illustration in the teaching of Pastor Van Sullivan of Lancaster, South Carolina.

The Word of God is the only thing that can revive us. Revival is the Word of God. I believe that in these last days, the Lord is pushing His Book, the Word of God to the forefront. Remember the story of the two men on the road to Emmaus. I tell you, friend, that was a long dusty walk home for them. These men felt everything they had believed and trusted in had died outside of Jerusalem three days before. They knew that Jesus had made a promise to rise on the third day, but they didn't see Him. So they just turned and headed home. Along the way, a stranger walked up and joined them. It was Jesus, but they did not recognize Him.

The stranger asked them one question. He asked, "Why is it that you are so sad along your way?" (see Lk. 24:17) Now these men were discouraged because Jesus had made a lot of promises, but they could not see the fruit of any of them at this time. I'm sure some Christians feel this way today; they are sad along their way. You may say, "They need a revival!" And you are right. Yet what they need is not in our idea of revival. These men responded to their companion's question by saying, "You *must* be a stranger in the city. Have you not heard about this one Jesus, who claimed to be the Messiah? He was killed, and He said He would rise again. We have heard He is risen, but we have not seen Him. And we are disgusted" (see Lk. 24:18-24).

The Lord realized that those boys needed to be revived. He also knew that only one thing would do it, and that one thing was the *Word of God*. So Jesus began with the prophets. He probably started all the way back with Moses. Then He probably moved on to Isaiah and pumped the Word of God into those men. I can almost picture their heads lifting up from their droopy, discouraged positions. And those souls that were tired, sad, and discouraged began to receive new life. A real revival is a revival of the Word of God. This is the true ministry of the Word.

By the time these men reached home, one of them realized, "My heart is on fire after talking to that man" (see Lk. 24:32). After that they didn't just sit down and take it easy now that they were revived. No! They jumped back on the road to go spread the Word and revive their brethren. That is what the Word will do in your heart. For if revival is only in our head or our feet it won't last long, but if you get it into your heart, two weeks, six months, even three years down the line, you will still be revived. The most important thing in the world is the Word of God. The answer to all problems is in the Word of God. I thank God for His marvelous Word and for men and women like Brother Van who preach God's Word without compromise.

Although God has declared that His Word is *His* power unto salvation (see Rom. 1:16), many are not experiencing that power and that salvation today. But by a mere *rumor* the ancient world was able to secure salvation. By a mere rumor of the Word, Rahab the harlot believed God and was able to procure salvation for her whole household and avoid the impending destruction. By the preaching of a believing Jewish girl, Naaman the Syrian leper was able to win salvation from the dreadful disease of leprosy. The power of God is forever present in the living Word of God, whether it is *rumored*, *preached*, or *exemplified*. God's Word will never go out and come back to Him void (see Is. 55:11). This is as true today as it ever was.

Many more still need to hear the *rumor* of the impending judgment on the human race. God still maintains that man shall not live by bread alone but by every Word that proceeds out of His mouth (see Mt. 4:4). The reason He sent His own Spirit to move on holy men was so that you and I may profit from His own very Word—Jesus Christ. The Word gives true doctrine, the Word reproves, corrects, and instructs in righteousness, so that we (those of us who are made children of the Most High by the Word) may be "perfect, thoroughly furnished unto all good works" (2 Tim. 3:16-17).

The Word of God is the *will of God* for you and me. Many are waiting to have visions from God. Others are waiting for dreams. Still others are waiting for an apparition to appear by their bedsides. Stop waiting, turn to the Word and to a true minister of the Word to receive instruction. Then God will increase and renew your strength. You will be able to mount up with wings like an eagle. (See Isaiah 40:19-31.) Turn to the ministry of the Word, that is the message that was preached to John the Baptist by the Word Himself. Yes faith comes by hearing and hearing by the Word of God.

The work of the pastor is to minister the Word of God from the pulpit, to spread the Word to those who have not yet heard it and become born again, and to be in prayer for those to whom he ministers so that they may receive all that God has for them through the ministry of the Word. This is a calling of which no one could be ashamed—to minister the living Word to the Body of Christ. Yet it is time that we, the rest of Christ's Body, begin to take up our calling in regard to ministering from the pews back to the pastor in the pulpit.

Chapter Four

Ministering From the Pews to the Pulpit and Its Rewards

But now hath God set the members every one of them in the body, as it hath pleased Him. ... That there should be no schism in the body; but that the members should have the same care one for another.

1 Corinthians 12:18,25

A Living Body Model

In the Church today, ministry is viewed as a one-way street—from the pulpit to the pews. This lopsided point of view comes from our inaccurate perception of the Body of Christ. Whenever we refer to the Body of Christ, we usually do not include the pastor. As a result, ministering to the Body often excludes the pastor, yet we still look to the pastor as *the* minister. It is not supposed to be this way. A careful examination of the operations of a body will reveal that the life of any body is dependent on the interdependence, interaction, and integration of all its functioning parts.

It is an awesome responsibility to subscribe to *being the Body of Christ* and "members in particular" (1 Cor. 12:27).

The failure of any member of a body to live up to its respective responsibility (not exercising its giftedness in the body) exposes the body to grave danger. No member of a body is placed there by God for merely cosmetic reasons. As a member of His Body, you have a particular responsibility in the Body of Christ. Many of us who subscribe to being members of the Body of Christ hardly know what we've gotten ourselves into! That is why there is so much irresponsibility in the church today.

"Now ye are the body of Christ, and members in particular" (1 Cor. 12:27) does not attest to the fact that Christ created a corpse, but a living organism that is an extension of Himself. Many of us are "vegetating" in the pews and not waking up to our respective responsibilities. All members of the same body are dependent on one another to exist. Their functions are synchronized to work with one another and for one another in unity for the common good of the body. There are absolutely no autonomous members; neither is there any form of cloning that will make all members perform the same function. Separate and distinct members of the body with respective functions or gifts must use their giftedness for the edification of the body.

> *If the foot shall say, Because I am not the hand, I am not of the body; is it therefore not of the body? And if the ear shall say, Because I am not the eye, I am not of the body; is it therefore not of the body? If the whole body were an eye, where were the hearing? If the whole were hearing, where were the smelling?*
>
> 1 Corinthians 12:15-17

Contrary to the necessary functioning of a body, we who claim to be the Body of Christ have held to the view that one of the members of this Body, the pastor, does not really need to be ministered to. This is a grave fallacy that must be corrected. If the members need to be ministered to by one part of the Body, the pastor, then we, in turn, must also minister to him or her for the common good of the Body. Anything less will put the whole Body in grave danger.

A Functioning Member:

In looking at the different parts of the body, it is important to note the purpose or function of each member. The hand is a gift to the body, and one will know the hand's function well enough at a time when one has no hands. The pastor is a gift from the Lord to the Church as the apostle Paul explains to the Ephesians:

> ...*When He ascended up on high, He led captivity captive, and gave gifts unto men.* ... *And He gave some, apostles; and some, prophets; and some, evangelists; and some, pastors and teachers;* [and the *purpose* was threefold] *for the perfecting of the saints, for the work of the ministry, for the edifying of the body of Christ.*
>
> Ephesians 4:8,11-12

The eye, for example, is a gift to the body. Its purpose is to *see* for the whole body. Spiritual gifts work in the same manner. When Jesus opened a blind man's eyes, people marveled and became excited by the miracle. However, they missed its purpose. Today, people pride themselves in being Christians, going to church, and being members of the church; yet they have downplayed the purpose of their membership in that assembly. From the Scriptures, we learn that

Jesus opened the blind man's eyes, "...That the works of God should be made manifest in him...[to reveal that] I am the light of the world" (Jn. 9:3,5).

When Jesus wanted to reveal Himself as the Resurrection and the Life, He called a dead man from his grave and raised him up from the dead. Jesus said, "...I am the resurrection, and the life: he that believeth in Me, though he were dead, yet shall he live" (Jn. 11:25). He fed 5,000 men, and maybe even a greater number of women and children with five loaves of bread and two fishes, but when the people requested more bread and a sign He told them, "You missed it; because 'I am the bread of life: he that cometh to Me shall never hunger; and he that believeth on Me shall never thirst' " (Jn. 6:35).

The operation of the gifts of the Holy Ghost are not the issue; they are the *purpose*. The operation of miracles is not to create a show; its purpose is to function as to get the attention of men, open their eyes, and draw men and women to the saving grace of Jesus Christ. The baptism of the Holy Ghost is not so you can go around shouting and speaking in tongues; its purpose was clearly explained by Jesus Christ:

> *But ye shall receive power, after that the Holy Ghost is come upon you: **and ye shall be witnesses unto Me** both in Jerusalem, and in all Judaea, and in Samaria, and **unto the uttermost part of the earth**.*
>
> Acts 1:8

Some claim to have the Holy Ghost, but they have never opened their mouths to witness to their neighbors of the saving grace of Jesus Christ. The Holy Ghost is not lazy! The Lord Himself testified of this:

*The Spirit of the Lord is upon Me, because He hath anointed Me **to preach the gospel** to the poor; He hath sent Me **to heal** the brokenhearted, **to preach deliverance** to the captives, and **recovering of sight** to the blind, **to set at liberty** them that are bruised, **to preach the acceptable year of the Lord**.*

Luke 4:18-19

Every gift has a purpose. The living Word of God, Jesus Christ Himself, is a gift for us and has a purpose. "For God so loved the world, that He gave His only begotten Son, that whosoever believeth in Him should not perish, but have everlasting life" (Jn. 3:16). Jesus is not for academic debates; He is the power of God unto salvation (see Rom. 1:16). Now it is time to ask yourself: "If I am a gift to the Body of Christ, what is my purpose in the Body? What is my purpose in the membership?" Could it be that the Lord put you there to work and support the pastor and His work in the local body?

*But now hath God set the members every one of them in the body, as it hath pleased Him. ... That there should be no schism in the body; but that the members should have the **same care one for another**.*

1 Corinthians 12:18,25

Now the hand has a gift for handling things. If the body needs things to be handled, it is imperative that the hand attends to this particular service. The eye has the gift of sight. When the body gets up in the morning and opens its eyelids, the eyes had better fulfill their responsibility to see for the body. As the body steps down from bed, it will need the feet and legs to fulfill their function so it can walk. In the same way the teeth are needed to chew the food; the stomach to digest it; the blood to carry the nutrients to the tissues and cells; the heart to pump the blood to be cleansed, or oxygenated, by the lungs. Every other organ is also needed in the body to perform its own respective function for the good (edification) of the body.

If one of its members refuses to function, the entire body will either be thrown into immediate danger or it will be unable to operate to its full potential. Even if one of the members simply refuses to function properly, the body will either die immediately or die a slow death as the body experiences one disabling incident after another. Every member of the body must use its gifts for the good of the body. However, what we see in our churches is that the pastor, a member of the Body, uses his gifts as a preacher and teacher for the good of everyone else, but hardly anyone considers using his or her gifts for the good of the pastor.

No single organ or cell in the body works for itself alone. In a way, each and every member feeds the body, and that member is itself fed by the rest of the body. The eyes feed the body with sight, and the body feeds the eyes with oxygen and nourishment through the blood. The ears feed the body through its gift of hearing, and the body feeds the ear with oxygen and nourishment through the blood. Each and every member plays a necessary part, and receives what it needs from the parts played by the rest of the body.

Consider what happens when one of the members of the body is sick. Let's use the eye for our example again. You may say, "Brother Toby, if one of the members is sick, then it needs a doctor." Okay, so we will get the best doctor money can buy. Even though the doctor performs the best possible laser surgery on that eye and prescribes the very best medication, he will still depend on *every member* in that body (the heart, the veins, the arteries, the nerves, etc.) to *work together in harmony* to effect the healing of that eye. The doctor, his surgery, and his medication of themselves will not effect one iota in the recovery of that eye! I'm sure you've heard of various transplants being rejected by the body into which the transplant was made? The problem was not the surgeon's work, the problem was the denial of the members to harmonize and work together with the new member. Therefore, an effective solution for healing or maintaining a healthy member and a healthy body involves the dedicated participation and working together of all the members of the body for its common good.

Translate this analogy back to the Body of Christ, and ask yourself, "Should ministry in the church be a one-way street? Should it flow from the pulpit to the pew only?" If we are sincere, we will agree that it should *not* be a one-way street. We will also agree that over the years we have done our pastors a great injustice. We have often viewed pastors, not as members of the Body, but just as "pastors"—detached from the Body having no problems, but a duty to take care of the Body.

This view has left pastors and their families crippled, in need, frustrated, lonely, and without anyone to turn to. Some have died in their need without anyone knowing of it because we are detached. Some have turned for help from their families and other pastors outside of their churches. But just as a sick body cannot be healed by the efforts of a doctor alone, the needs of that pastor shall never be fully met by another pastor or a family member without the full cooperation and intervention of the members of his local church.

> *But now hath God set the members every one of them in the body, as it hath pleased Him. ... That there should be no schism in the body; but that the members should have the same care one for another.*
>
> 1 Corinthians 12:18,25

> *For as the body is one, and hath many members, and all the members of that one body, being many, are one body: so also is Christ.*
>
> 1 Corinthians 12:12

Now, as members of the Body we have failed to do our part in the Great Commission. There is schism in the Body. If the eyes want to walk, the feet want to see, the teeth refuses to chew food, and the heart refuses to pump blood, then death for the body is imminent. We have failed to support those who are called to preach the gospel. This problem needs to be addressed immediately. A drastic medical problem calls for a drastic solution because of its life and death consequences. Please pray, and after all the praying, do your duty. Minister to your pastor!

The solution for the pastor's problem is not through addresses from pulpit to pulpit, or clergy to clergy. It is time to address this problem from the pews to the pulpit. The solution is not simply in pastors' conferences, or group meetings the bulk of the solution is within the local assembly where every lively stone is fitly joined together to build that spiritual house. The key is for each member to understand his or her own responsibility and make it a personal duty to fulfill that responsibility so that the pastor can fully attend to the ministry of the Word and of prayer.

A quotation from Charles G. Finney's *Revival of Religion* illustrates this principle:

God employs you to sell goods as His Clerk, and your minister He employs to teach His Children, and He requires you to pay the salary [of the minister] out of the income of the store. Now, do you call this your sacrifice, and say that you are making a great sacrifice to pay this minister's salary? No: you are just as much bound to sell goods for God as he is to preach for God. You have no more right to sell goods for the purpose of laying up money than he has to preach the gospel for the same purpose. You are bound to be as pious, aim as singly at the glory of God, in selling goods, as he is in preaching the gospel. And thus you are as fully to give up your whole time for the service of God as he does. You and your family may lawfully live out of the profits of this store, and so may the minister and his family, just as lawfully. If you sell goods from these motives, selling goods is just as much serving God as preaching; and a man who sells goods on these principles, and acts in conformity to them, is just as pious—just as much in the service of God—as he is who preaches the gospel. Every man is bound to serve God in his calling; the minister by teaching, the merchant by selling goods; the farmer by tilling his field; and the lawyer and the physician by applying the duties of their professions. It is equally unlawful for any one of these to labor for meat that perishes. All they do is to be for God, and all they earn, after comfortably supporting their families is to be dedicated to the spread of the Gospel and the salvation of the world (USA, Revivals of Religion, by Fleming H. Revell Company, p. 277).

Supporting Your Pastor, A Hidden Treasure

Ministering to your pastor is designed by our heavenly Father in Heaven to be a means of blessing His children while they are here on earth and to store up blessings for the life to come. Unfortunately, many Christians consider it bad news that the propagation of the gospel is 100 percent dependent on the practice of giving. The Lord chose to make it this way; therefore, it *must* be good for us! Yet many of us are still not excited about giving, and only a selected few have tapped into the treasure God has provided and are financing the spread of the gospel.

Too many Christians have believed the devil's lies and ended up being robbed of the blessings that come from ministering to men and women of God. By refusing to minister, these Christians are forever shortchanged, and consequently they suffer lack in their own lives on a consistent basis. By being disobedient to the commands of our Lord, even if it is by ignorance, these Christians are withholding the portion God has claimed for His servants who minister before Him. Their refusal to give and bless the men and women of God has stopped up the windows of Heaven that God desires to open up in their own lives.

Your heavenly Father has unselfishly designed ministering to your pastor as a means of opening the hidden treasures of ministering the gospel to us who are not called to preach. Although this may appear to be a strong statement, our Lord clearly taught that if you receive (materially support or minister to) a prophet in the name of a prophet, you shall receive a prophet's reward (see Mt. 10:41). He followed this statement by saying,

And whosoever shall give to drink unto one of these little ones a cup of cold water only in the name of a disciple, verily I say unto you, he shall in no wise lose his reward.

Matthew 10:42

The Lord could have designed things in such a way that His disciples would be fed with manna from Heaven. He could have chosen to use ravens to feed them as he did with Elijah (see 1 Kings 17:1-7). Yet even after God used ravens to feed Elijah, He still decided to meet the needs of the woman in Zarephath who was preparing to die by giving her the opportunity to receive the rewards of ministering to a man of God. Clearly God provides His children with the opportunity to minister to His servants so that we may enjoy the benefits of ministering the Word of God even though we may not carry the title of a minister ourselves.

The rewards and benefits embedded in this truth are immense, and the devil knows it. The closest biblical comparison can only be made by combining the biblical promises regarding tithing with the practice of godly giving of offerings, yet this is a very special type of giving. Providing for the needs of a man of God carries with it an earthly and heavenly reward greater than any prosperity doctrine drawn from the holy Scriptures. And as Paul declared, "If in this life only

53

we have hope in Christ, we are of all men most miserable" (1 Cor. 15:19). What a heavenly hope therefore, to provide for the pastor and his family in the name of Christ Jesus.

However, the enemy, the devil, from ages long gone until this present moment, desires to bury this truth from the sight of every child of God. He wants to rob the Body of Christ of its rightful spiritual and material prosperity. In my opinion (which is substantiated by the Word of God), providing for the needs of a man of God carries with it an earthly and heavenly reward and far exceeds that of any doctrine on prosperity that is drawn from the Holy Scriptures. The promises of reward for tithing and giving do not approach the depth of Christ's statement, "He that receiveth a prophet in the name of a prophet shall receive a prophet's reward" (Mt. 10:41a). The promise for tithing is "I will...open the windows of heaven, and pour you out a blessing, that there shall not be room enough to receive it" (Mal. 3:10b). And the promise for giving is, "Give, and it shall be given unto you; good measure, pressed down, and shaken together, and running over, shall *men* give into your bosom" (Lk. 6:38a). The promises of rewards from tithing are from Heaven to us on earth. They are, therefore, earthbound. The promise of rewards from giving are from men to the giver. They are also earthbound. But the promised rewards for supporting a minister of the gospel includes all the above plus some future heavenly reward that has not yet been quantified nor can it be quantified by man.

I think I like the last reward better than the others because the Holy Spirit says, "If in this life only we have hope in Christ, we are of all men most miserable" (1 Cor. 15:19). What a heavenly hope it is, therefore, to provide for the pastor and his family in the name of Christ Jesus. We are promised we will receive a prophet's reward, but we don't know exactly what it is. We can see a glimpse of the earthly reward when we look at the lives of those who took it upon themselves to minister to the prophets, God's servants, like Elijah, Elisha, David, Jeremiah, the Lord Jesus, and Paul. Paul declared to the Philippians who had ministered to him:

> *But my God shall supply all your need according to His riches* [souls saved as a result of your gifts for the sake of the gospel] *in glory by Christ Jesus.*
>
> Philippians 4:19

We experience needs in this life on earth only. In Heaven we will have no needs. So according to the enrichment of Heaven with the souls touched by your sacrificial giving to those working in the gospel ministry, God Almighty shall supply *all your needs*. This Scripture cannot be claimed by everyone. It may be claimed only by those who have provided for the needs of the man of God, as the Philippian saints did for Paul. That is why Paul addressed the Philippian saints,

> *...ye sent once and again unto my necessity. Not because I desire a gift: but I desire fruit that may* **abound to your account.** *But I have all, and abound: I am full, having received...the things which were sent from you,* **an odour of a sweet smell, a sacrifice acceptable, wellpleasing to God.**
>
> Philippians 4:16-18

Therefore, it is a gift to God, not just the pastor, when we provide for the needs of the pastor. Our actions are actually building a savings deposit in Heaven (His riches in glory) that will abound to our account when we stand in judgment. We also know that no income on earth could ever compensate for value of the minister's work; neither can our reward for supporting our pastors be measured in earthly terms.

Consider also this additional promise from the Lord:

...Verily I say unto you, There is no man that hath left house, or brethren, or sisters, or father, or mother, or wife, or children, or lands [that is sacrificed], *for My sake* [salvation], *and the gospel's, but he shall receive an hundredfold now in this time* [in this life], *houses, and brethren, and sisters, and mothers, and children, and lands, with persecutions; and in the world to come eternal life.*

Mark 10:29-30

Many of us left the world for the Lord's sake when we became saved; however, we have remained indifferent to supporting ministers of the gospel. Essentially, we are refusing to leave the world for the gospel's sake. We have gained the whole world at the expense of lost souls. We forget the Lord's charge to His Church, you and me, to go preach the gospel to every creature (see Mk. 16:15). Again, you may not be a preacher, but as you send out a preacher with your gifts, your feet will be as beautiful as the one who brings the glad tidings of the gospel (see Is. 52:7; Rom. 10:15).

And how shall they preach, except they be sent? as it is written, How beautiful are the feet of them that preach the gospel of peace, and bring glad tidings of good things!

Romans 10:15

"How shall they preach, except they be sent?" Was God asking Himself this question? Is God telling us that He must send a preacher? No! Have you not read in the Book of Acts of how the Church prayed, and as a result they sent Paul and Barnabas forth to go minister the gospel (see Acts 13:1-4)? It was the Church that was obliged to send the preacher to the unsaved. The Lord commanded the preacher to go empty-handed, but He also obliged the Church to provide the preacher with the worth of his hire. Now, when the preacher goes, the sender goes with him; therefore, the preacher's beautiful feet are also the sender's beautiful feet, and the preacher's reward is also the sender's reward.

Have we ever asked ourselves what the Lord expected of the servant given one talent (see Mt. 25:14-30)? Here we see the ever astonishing truth of the Scriptures. By His parable the Lord showed that He expected as much increase from the servant with one talent as He did from the one with five talents. You may never be a preacher, an evangelist, or a teacher. But as Christians, we all have that gift of eternal life. We all have received the charge to take the gospel to every creature. Most importantly, we all have the gift of the Holy Ghost by whom we were brought to Christ. And anyone with that gift needs to act in accordance with the same Jesus who declared:

The Spirit of the Lord is upon Me, because He hath anointed Me to preach the gospel to the poor; He hath sent Me to heal the brokenhearted, to preach deliverance to the captives, and recovering of sight to the blind, to set at liberty them that are bruised, to preach the acceptable year of the Lord.

Luke 4:18-19

You can still be a pastor without pastoring, a teacher without teaching, and an evangelist without leaving your home church. You can actually acquire the respective rewards of a pastor, an evangelist, and a teacher through your ministry and material support of these ministers and their families.

The devil knows all this, and he wants you and me to continue in our limited vision. He does not want souls to be saved, and he does not want the Word to reach our ears and cause us to have faith in the living God.

Satan has dared to squirm through our church walls to prevent you and I from hearing the Lord's command and learning of the benefits we will receive for our obedience. These are the promises of the King of kings and the Lord of lords. He is faithful and able to perform exceeding abundantly above what we could ask or think (see Eph. 3:20). God will not be unrighteous to forget your good work and labors of love that you have showed toward His name in your ministering to the saints and to those who minister (see Heb. 6:10). Let's reclaim our ground. Amen!

To underscore the importance of providing for His ministers, the Lord promises a reward to anyone who takes it upon him or herself to give a cup of cold water to anyone only because that someone is a disciple:

And whosoever shall give to drink unto one of these little ones a cup of cold water only in the name of a disciple, verily I say unto you, he shall in no wise lose his reward.

Matthew 10:42

A cup of water! The Lord is not stressing the importance of water in the verse, but that of *giving the least thing* to

58

someone simply because that person is a minister of the gospel. Throughout most of the world, especially in Africa, water is that commodity that travelers are guaranteed to receive free. African tradition will permit someone to get away with not providing food to a stranger but the cultural rules will not excuse anyone who fails to provide a stranger with water. Even if a traveler has to pay for his food, water is always free. If the Lord will reward us for providing what is considered free and covers two-thirds of the earth's surface, think of how much more He will reward us when we fulfill our responsibilities in providing for pastors things that are less readily available and more expensive, such as food, clothing, tuition for the children, housing, transportation, and other things.

The Lord had more to say about ministering and providing for His disciples than He had to say about almsgiving and tithing combined! He knew some of the tithes would be locked up in some board committee in situations when a stingy person's decision would leave the pastor and his family in a state of perpetual need. He knew the time would come when certain churches would have swelling bank accounts while the pastor would be struggling under a great load of pressures, needs, bills, and the decision to stay on or quit the ministry. That is why He instituted the ministry of giving to disciples, which He accompanied with unparalleled benefits. That is why salaries should only serve as the beginning of providing for the pastor's monthly needs—not the end! Each member should take personal interest and make it his or her personal responsibility to ensure that the pastor is free of any needs. Every church member should stay conscientiously aware of the part that he or she plays in the welfare of the pastor.

The Lord places such great emphasis on this subject that He almost gave away Heaven for it. Our Lord Jesus Christ, who would not even bend a toe at the promise of the earth from the devil, practically bent over backwards to make it clear in Scripture that we are to care for His pastors. Why are these servants so close to His heart? Jesus values His pastors so much because they are on the very mission that He left glory for, the salvation of our souls. Who in a secular business would throw out a promise to his employees that sounds like: "He who receives a Director in the name of a Director will receive a Director's salary"? That person would soon go bankrupt! But that is just what the Lord did on behalf of His pastors and ministers of the gospel!

> *He that receiveth a prophet in the name of a prophet shall receive a prophet's reward; and he that receiveth a righteous man in the name of a righteous man shall receive a righteous man's reward.*
>
> Matthew 10:41

That's quite a promise—unless the Lord does not mean what He says. But the Scriptures have the answer to this as well: "God forbid: yea, let God be true, but every man a liar" (Rom. 3:4a). Of course, God means what He is saying here! And if I am reading it correctly, what it seems to be saying is that the entire Church is being offered the opportunity to receive a minister's reward even though we all can't be ministers!

The devil knows all this, and he wants you and me to continue in our limited vision. He does not want souls to be saved; nor does he want the Word to reach our ears and cause us to have faith in the living God. The devil is fighting his hardest to keep this truth from disseminating throughout the Church of God, the pillar and ground of truth (see 1 Tim. 3:15b). His ploy robs the saints of the knowledge and benefits God bestows upon those who make the least effort to practice this divine command. The devil wants to prevent you and me from hearing the Lord's command that if we minister to those who serve as ministers to God, we will receive the reward of a minister. This is a promise from the King of kings and the Lord of lords to those He loves so much He gave His life for them. Jesus could not have been lying! He is faithful and able to perform exceedingly abundantly above what we ask or think (see Eph. 3:20). "[He] is not unrighteous to forget your [good] work and labour of love, which ye have shewed toward His name, in that ye have ministered to the saints, and do minister" (Heb. 6:10). Let's reclaim our ground. Amen.

Chapter Five

Worshiping in Giving

When considering the subject of supporting our pastors, it is proper to make a brief study on the subject of *giving*; for it is through the avenue of giving that we will properly minister to our pastors. There exists a vast amount of misunderstanding and/or ignorance on this subject, and this is the main reason both pastors and members of our churches are suffering lack today. But giving is the door to freedom. Contrary to what our psyche will have us think and believe, "that to give is to end up with less," giving creates *more* for the giver's advantage than is experienced by either the non-giver or the receiver.

The Word thus instructs that it is more blessed to give than to receive (see Acts 20:35). Even God Himself so loved the world that He *gave* His only begotten Son, so that whoever will believe on Him will not need to perish, but will receive eternal life (see Jn. 3:16). Because the Lord gave, He opened the gate for multitudes to enter Heaven. If He had not given, man would not only still be destitute in his sin, but Heaven would be inaccessible to man today. For we know that though He was rich, yet for our sake He became poor so that by His poverty we might become rich (see 2 Cor. 8:9).

Giving is a barometer of love. The highest score on this barometer was reached through the death of the *only* begotten Son of the great Giver, Jehovah-Jireh, "the Lord our provider." "Greater love hath no man than this, that a man *lay down* his life for his friend" (Jn. 15:13). And, "Behold, what manner of love the Father hath bestowed upon us [*by His giving*], that we should be called the sons of God..." (1 Jn. 3:1). The Old Testament shadow demonstrated this through Abraham's offering of his only seed as a gift and a sacrifice to the Father. Because of this, the Lord promised and said,

> *...By Myself have I sworn...for because thou hast done this thing, and hast not withheld thy son,* [but given] *thine only son:* **that in blessing I will bless thee, and in multiplying I will multiply thy seed as the stars of the heaven, and as the sand which is upon the sea shore; and thy seed shall possess the gates of his enemies;** *and in thy seed shall all the nations of the earth be blessed; because thou hast obeyed My voice.*

> Genesis 22:16-18.

What greater lesson than this could we ask to learn from the Word of God in regards to giving? Very simply stated, giving will bring blessings to the giver, and through giving, the giver will serve as God's agent of blessing to others. Giving that satisfies the will of God always receives the commendation of God and a generous reciprocity from God. It is to this effect that the Lord promised to the one who gives,

> *Give, and it shall be given unto you; good measure, pressed down, and shaken together, and running over,*

64

shall men give into your bosom. For with the same measure that ye mete withal it shall be measured to you again.

Luke 6:38

God gives you His love so that you can reflect it unto others. God blesses you so that you can be a blessing to others. God loved us so much that He gave all He had. As His ambassadors we need to reflect the character of God. And one of His qualities is giving. When we close our eyes to the needy, we end up needing ourselves. When we close our eyes to the needy, we fail to reflect the love of God. The love of God in our hearts is not addressed to us; it is addressed to the world for whom the Lord died. Giving is a grace gift, which is bestowed upon us by God. It is not something we have to do on our own. It is something God will do if we allow Him. I have often heard individuals say that we should give until it hurts. If it hurts, it is not done by the Spirit. For giving cannot be done by might or by power; it can only be done by His Spirit (see Mic. 3:8). The cheerful giver that the Lord loves (see 2 Cor. 9:7) cannot be hurting or grudging at the same time!

Giving is designed to be a privilege so that ministers may spread the gospel and that the poor may be relieved of their suffering. This does not exclude the poor or the minister from giving. For in truth, the practice of giving will bring many of the poor out of poverty. Giving is an honored service bestowed by God to His children, and it should not only be revered but constantly practiced. This duty is not merely for the wealthy but also for the poor and those with modest means.

Giving Is Spiritual

Pastor Jack Hayford said it well when he said, "If there is a word that makes us want to run, that word is *give*."

Unfortunately for many Christians, *give* is a "switch-off" word that immediately pulls them down from the glory of high spiritual worship back to the soulish realm of rationalization. The word *give* will usually send that wake-up call, that rational demon scurrying down our spinal cord, reminding us to come back to reality. This is why someone once declared that our pocketbooks and wallets need to be baptized! Giving, and especially material giving, is a nerve-touching issue to many believers. Our rational faculties have successfully debated with our faith and taught us that to give is to be left with less. But with Christians, it is imperative that giving should come from the heart, as opposed to the head. It should be mixed with faith rather than rationalization.

Giving is and should always be done in worship of the Giver. Prayer should predicate and govern all acts of worshipful giving. Giving belongs to the spiritual rather than the rational medium, because they that worship Him must worship Him in spirit and in truth (see Jn. 4:24). The Bible says, "For he that soweth to his flesh shall of the flesh reap corruption; but he that soweth to the Spirit shall of the Spirit reap life everlasting" (Gal. 6:8). In this little parable, sowing applies specifically to the need of feeding and maintaining the ministers of the gospel. "He that soweth to the Spirit" implies that the person who supports the teachers of God's Word does a spiritual work and shall reap life everlasting. And "he that soweth to his flesh," implies that the person who gives nothing to the ministers of God's Word and only feeds and cares for himself, his flesh, shall of the flesh reap corruption, not only in the present life but also in the life to come. Giving to the Lord's work is, therefore, a spiritual activity, and it should be done in fervent worship of the Father.

The sunset of *giving* should be a sunrise of praise and glory to Jehovah-Jireh for the great things He has done in using us to be a very present help in time of need. Paul says, "But I have all, and abound: I am full, having received of Epaphroditus the things which were sent from you, an odour of a sweet smell, a sacrifice acceptable, wellpleasing to God" (Phil. 4:18). What a commendation for someone who worships in giving! His giving is a sweet fragrance before the King of kings! His giving is *a sacrifice acceptable* to the Lord of lords! His sacrifice is *wellpleasing* to the Alpha and Omega, and especially so when the giver directs this giving to the minister of the gospel!

Named as one of the gifts of the Holy Ghost, giving or generosity has been locked away in a nickel-hard safe by those of us who are Pentecostals while we amplify speaking in tongues as the initial evidence of the baptism of the Holy Ghost. We have often made this manifestation the initial and final evidence of the work of the Holy Ghost in our lives. We have failed to mention the second, third, fourth, fifth manifestations, much less the actual fruit of the Holy Ghost. I have never read in the Bible of a selfish or lazy Holy Ghost, yet we who claim to be baptized with the Holy Ghost have, unlike the early Church, never opened our mouths in witness for the gospel or lifted a single finger in support of the gospel. But the evidence from the Word declares that the early saints sold their estates and laid the money at the apostles' feet for the preaching of the gospel and for the needs of the saints. This they did with joy and simplicity, thus manifesting the character of Jesus Christ (the fruit of the Spirit).

Don't be deceived, God is not mocked (see Gal. 6:7)! When you despise the needy, when you despise the ministers of the gospel, you are despising God. For He has ordained that those who preach the gospel shall live by the gospel (see 1 Cor. 9:14).

When you are providing for the needy by giving, you are actually honoring and acknowledging God, Jehovah-Jireh, as your provider. Consider Abraham's response to his son when he asked where the lamb was for the burnt offering: "My son, God will provide Himself a lamb for a burnt offering" (see Gen. 22:7-8). Stepping into giving as a form of worship makes giving an act of faith ("Abraham believed God" [Rom. 4:3]) and not an act of *rationality*! This throws off a lot of people, and it is the major hindrance of the "giving" form of worship.

But just as we must compare apples with apples, we must compare spiritual things with spiritual. At the end of giving, ask yourself two questions: "Who is being glorified?" and "Who is being blessed?" In answer to these two questions, a wrongful motive of giving will ascribe glory to self and blessings to the recipient. A right motive of giving will ascribe glory to God Almighty, the Provider of all things, and blessings to the giver because it is more blessed to give than to receive. All Christians are admonished and expected to give. It is a fundamental duty of all Christians—poor and rich, young and old, man and woman—with no exception. We are the salt of the earth (see Mt. 5:13), and it is our responsibility to season and preserve every human life here on earth through our giving for the work of the gospel.

Giving for the Gospel Is Banking in Heaven

Man's fundamental needs can be divided into two basic headings—the need for human existence and the need for spiritual existence. The world system is too preoccupied with the need for human existence. The world is busy chasing after this need, while completely forgetting the other. Believers have fallen into the same trap. They are busy acquiring and accumulating goods that will profit the flesh, but they are neglecting to store up treasure for themselves in Heaven.

> *Lay not up for yourselves treasures upon earth, where moth and rust doth corrupt, and where thieves break through and steal: but lay up for yourselves treasures in heaven, where neither moth nor rust doth corrupt, and where thieves do not break through nor steal: for where your treasure is, there will your heart be also.*
>
> Matthew 6:19-21

Let's "...Take heed, and beware of covetousness: for a man's life consisteth not in the abundance of the things which he possesseth" (Lk. 12:15). We must do as our Lord admonished us,

> *But seek ye first the kingdom of God, and His righteousness; and all these things shall be added unto you. Take therefore no thought for the morrow: for the morrow shall take thought for the things of itself. Sufficient unto the day is the evil thereof.*
>
> Matthew 6:33-34

The Lord told satan, the prince of this world, "...Man shall not live by bread alone, but by every word that proceedeth out of the mouth of God" (Mt. 4:4). This is spiritual food, and man has significantly neglected it. That is why Jesus came to earth; He is the Bread of Life. And "He that hath the Son hath life; and he that hath not the Son of God hath not life" (1 Jn. 5:12). This is the reason Jesus left glory to descend into a human body—that we may have Bread of Life. Is this reason not good enough for us (we who have this Bread) to support those chosen to take this Bread to others? If taking this Bread of Life to mankind was important enough for the Father to spare not His own Son, you better believe that He will recompense any person who spares nothing for himself so that God's Word will go out.

Reflect again upon these words of our Savior:

*...Verily I say unto you, There is no man that hath left house, or brethren, or sisters, or father, or mother, or wife, or children, or lands, for my sake, and **the gospel's**, but he shall **receive an hundredfold now in this time**, houses, and brethren, and sisters, and mothers, and children, and lands, **with persecutions**; and in the world to come eternal life. But many that are first shall be last; and the last first.*

Mark 10:29-31

You have left the world for the Lord's sake by being saved. You no longer do the things you used to do. You don't steal; rather, you attend church and sing in the choir. But have you also left the world for the gospel's sake? Are you giving for the propagation of the gospel? If you have been missing out on many hundredfold blessings, it is because you performed just one part of the commandment and neglected the other. But the promise is to those that have left for our Lord's sake *and* the gospel's.

Every child of God is supposed to have two bank accounts, an earthly one to meet his earthly needs and a spiritual one to meet the needs of the propagation of the gospel. I dare you to feed the gospel account and see how the Lord will feed your earthly account! Paul declared to the Philippians that he had no need for them to give to him. However, he encouraged them by stating that their giving to him was actually feeding their account in Heaven!

*Now ye Philippians know also, that in the beginning of the gospel, when I departed from Macedonia, no church communicated with me as concerning giving and receiving, but ye only. For even in Thessalonica ye sent once and again unto my necessity. **Not because I desire a gift**: but I desire fruit that may **abound to your account**.*

Philippians 4:15-17

And because of their giving, Paul, inspired by the Holy Spirit, promised, "But my God shall supply all your need according to His riches [souls saved as a result of your giving] in glory by Christ Jesus" (Phil. 4:19).

Do you have a bank account on earth for the sole purpose of saving souls? If not, do you truly love the Father or do you love the material things you are hanging onto?

Love not the world, neither the things that are in the world. If any man love the world, the love of the Father is not in him. For all that is in the world, the lust of the flesh, and the lust of the eyes, and the pride of

71

life, is not of the Father, but is of the world. And the world passeth away, and the lust thereof: but he that doeth the will of God abideth for ever.

1 John 2:15-17

The Lord said, "My meat is to do the will of My Father" (see Jn. 4:34). The Lord's meat should also be our meat, for we are His Body. Open an account not only for the earthly "self," but also to do the will of the Father for the salvation of souls.

The Secret About Possessions

Who is the owner of what we are giving away? A good understanding of the owner of what we "possess" will give and maintain in us a right perspective of giving. An *owner* is the person who holds the legal title to a property. It can also refer to the person of highest rank or authority. Drawing from these two definitions, we can establish right away that the Lord Jesus Christ holds the legal title on each of us who ascribes to belonging to the Body of Christ by being born again. We were bought with a price, and we are not our own (see 1 Cor. 6:19-20).

Our problems on earth have persisted because we own too much of ourselves and have merely given the Lord lip service and little else of ourselves. Because we own too much of ourselves, we are motivated to act out of self-preservation, and actions motivated by self-preservation are selfish and egocentric. Out of this motive we will embrace the principle of "the survival of the fittest." However being governed by this type of principle is unprofitable for our lives as Christians. We are "rich," yet "poor." We are "blind," but we think we can see (see Rev. 3:17).

Anyone who seeks to save his life will lose it (see Lk. 17:33). This refers to living by the dictates of the soul and the flesh, and we know this will not bring glory in the presence of God Almighty. But a life of the Spirit seeks to bring forth more life by seeking to save that which is lost. This kind of person will give, sacrifice, and deny self at every turn so as to give another person the opportunity to *live*.

> *Let this mind be in you, which was also in Christ Jesus: who, being in the form of God, thought it not robbery to be equal with God: but made Himself of no reputation, and took upon Him the form of a servant, and was made in the likeness of men: and being found in fashion as a man, He humbled Himself, and became obedient unto death, even the death of the cross.*
>
> Philippians 2:5-8

The Word is Spirit and life. The Word says, "Give." Therefore, there must be life in giving! Let us, therefore, obey the Spirit and be led by the Spirit; and we will not fulfill the lust of the flesh, which is contrary to God (see Gal. 5:16).

In essence, everything that we "own" is not really ours. The earth is the Lord's and the fullness thereof (see 1 Cor. 10:26), and so is all the gold and the cattle on a thousand hills (see Ps. 50:10). All is the Lord's. So although we think of ourselves quite highly as authors of whatever we may give to others, God is actually both our owner and the author of everything we have and all we give away. We were naked when He brought us into this world, and nothing we "possess" is actually ours. Job said, "The Lord gave, and the Lord hath taken away..." (Job 1:21b). All things are of the Lord and for the Lord. We are only custodians or stewards in charge of the things we possess as well as the temple of the Holy Spirit, our physical bodies. And someday we will be required to give an account of our stewardship to the Owner of all things.

> *Wherefore we labour, that, whether present or absent, we may be accepted of Him. For we must all appear before the judgment seat of Christ; that every one may receive the things done in His body, according to that He hath done, whether it be good or bad.*
>
> 2 Corinthians 5:9-10

As custodians, or stewards, we are suppose to multiply our "talents" and not bury them in the ground (see Mt. 25:14-30). For the Lord, the Sower of the seed, desires to have us make an increase so that we may in turn bless others.

> *As it is written: "He has scattered abroad His gifts to the poor; His righteousness endures forever." Now he who supplies seed to the sower and bread for food will also supply and increase your store of seed and will enlarge the harvest of your righteousness. **You will be made rich** in every way **so that you can be generous** on every occasion, and through us your generosity will result in thanksgiving to God.*
>
> 2 Corinthians 9:9-11 NIV

Now, knowing that we are not our own, we should be assured that the person who can best make use of us and all that we have is the person who designed and placed us into the Body. You are the Lord's, so whatever job you are doing and whatever you own, you need to view it as an assignment or property from the Lord. He has a specific reason and plan for assigning you what you have.

Now we see why the Church behaved as they did in the first century:

And the multitude of them that believed were of one heart and of one soul: neither said any of them that ought of the things which he possessed was his own; but they had all things common. And with great power gave the apostles witness of the resurrection of the Lord Jesus: and great grace was upon them all. Neither was there any among them that lacked: for as many as were possessors of lands or houses sold them, and brought the prices of the things that were sold, and laid them down at the apostles' feet: and distribution was made unto every man according as he had need. And Joses, who by the apostles was surnamed Barnabas, (which is, being interpreted, The son of consolation,) a Levite, and of the country of Cyprus, having land, sold it, and brought the money, and laid it at the apostles' feet.

Acts 4:32-37

If the angel of death that delivered God's judgment upon Ananias and Sapphira was to visit our churches, the witness of Western and worldly individualism would keep him very busy converting our churches into mortuaries. And in the face of such judgment, truly, would any of us survive?

As was noted in the quote from Charles Finney in Chapter Four, God has employed you to work at your job, while He has employed your minister to teach His children the gospel. God requires that you take care of the minister out of the income of your employment. You are just as bound to work for your employer for God as the pastor is to preach for God.

And just as you and your family may legitimately live out of the profits of working for your employer, so may the minister and his family just as legitimately be permitted to expect to live off the fruits of ministering for the Lord. All that each man does should be done for God. Therefore after each person has paid his or her tithes and met the general needs of his or her families, the rest of the individual's income should be dedicated to the spread of the gospel and to the salvation of the world. Yet how far short of this does each of us fall?

Our Mathematics Is Not Equal to God's Mathematics

Once you understand that giving is (or should be) a spiritual thing and that you neither own your body nor whatever "possessions" that have been entrusted to you, you must alter your perceptions regarding your actions as a child of God. "But the natural man receiveth not the things of the Spirit of God: for they are foolishness unto him: neither can he know them, because they are spiritually discerned" (1 Cor. 2:14). Our fears and reason have been in contrast and direct opposition to the truth of God, for they have taught us that to give is to be left with less. For the economy of God as it is expressed by His Spirit in the Word presents a different kind of mathematics by saying that it is more blessed to give than to receive. As children of God who should be walking by the Spirit, we must learn the rules of this other kind of math— the walk of faith. To the soul this mathematics is awkward and strange. The rules of these mathematics are far different than the methods of "$1 + 1 = 2$" that the soul has used ever since preschool. In the School of Faith, $1 + 1 = 1$. For this reason shall a man leave his father and mother and cleave unto his wife and they two shall be one (see Eph. 5:31).

As high as the heavens are above the earth, so are God's thoughts above our thoughts (see Is. 55:9). You can scratch your head all you want, but you will never figure out how a thousand years can be like one day and one day like a thousand years (see 2 Pet. 3:8). Here in the world of the Father's own math, Paul (a longtime resident) will tell you to call those things that be not as though they were (see Rom. 4:17). The soul will deny this spiritual principle with much kicking and screaming. Yet the prophets of old who ventured to use this spiritual mathematical principle can attest that through it one of us can chase a thousand and two of us can chase ten thousand (see Deut. 32:30). The great prophet Elisha could confirm the spiritual principles of God's mathematics. By his faith he could look at a fierce host of horses and chariots of an angry Syrian king and assure his servant, "Fear not: for they that be with us are more than they that be with them" (2 Kings 6:16). This same prophet satisfied 100 men with 20 loaves of bread (see 2 Kings 4:42-44).

It is in the world of God's mathematics that we already have the "*substance* of things hoped for" and the "*evidence* of things" *not yet* seen. This is strange and odd to the soul, and it may be confusing to many, but not to the spirit that walks after the Father's mathematics. Here in the Father's mathematical world the laws of nature (which are actually the natural laws of God) are defied. The natural, mathematical laws of astrophysics may say the sun will never stand still, but Joshua, who lived in the world of the Lord's own mathematics, can testify to astrophysicists that not only can He cause the sun to stand still but He also leveled a whole city wall without lifting a finger—only a shout. Shall I end without making mention of Elisha who could tell you that an ax head does float in water? The Lord Himself will tell you that you can walk on water and feed 5,000 men, not counting women and children, with two loaves of bread and two fishes and still have more bread and more fish left than what you started with. He will tell you that faith the size of a mustard seed will do what cases of dynamite cannot do—move a mountain and place it in the sea. Jonah will tell you that you can live in the belly of a big fish for three days without actually becoming its lunch, its breakfast, or its dinner, and that after you emerge you will still be able to make a three-day journey in only one day. Shadrach, Meshach, and Abednego will tell you that $1 + 1 + 1 = 4$ and that there is no strength in a fiery furnace, yet that same furnace can still consume arbitrators of the physical realm.

It's a whole new world, my friend. If you want to live in this world of God's spiritual mathematics, you will be living by a very different set of rules. There is, for example, one stating you must die in order to live (see Jn. 12:24). You must also believe *before* you see (see Jn. 20:25-29). And as awkward as it may sound, you will have to "put the cart before the horse" because we have thought of things the other way around for too long. You will have to give before you will receive. And you too will have to believe that $1 + 1 + 1 = 4$. That Babylonian king may have seen three go into the fiery furnace, but the three Hebrew boys knew that there was a fourth man—the One they worshipped. Your Nebuchadnezzar may soon be seeing a fourth man, but you will be able to state that that's what you've been trying to tell him all along. We have the evidence and the substance even though we may not see it!

Yes, as high as the heavens are above the earth, so high are His thoughts above our thoughts. It is a challenge for every child of God to learn these different set of rules. The earlier he learns them, the better things will be for him and the sooner he will save himself from a lot of trouble in these perilous times. These are just a few of the rules that apply to giving. Yes indeed, it *is* more blessed to give than to receive. Get this truth into every area of your being. It is good medicine for life on earth.

Giving Symbolized:

Giving is often typified in the Word of God by the sowing and reaping practices of farmers. The rewards of the farmer's labor are abundantly evident during the reaping of harvest time. The same is true of the labor of the indwelling Holy Ghost. If we allow Him to work in our lives as children of God, there will be a great harvest of the fruit of the Holy Ghost. "Wherefore by their fruits ye shall know them" (Mt. 7:20). If a person claims to be a farmer yet never cultivates the land or sows but still expects a harvest, he will be left expecting for a long time. If he eats all his previous harvest and tries to plant leftovers or just any kind of seed, he will reap very sparingly. But if he picks the choicest of the seeds, labors, and prepares the soil well, does his planting at the appropriate time, and the Lord of glory favors the farmer with good weather, then that farmer will have his barns filled when harvest time comes.

Sowing invariably is accompanied by expectation of harvest. No farmer plants without the expectation of harvesting. Now the Bible teaches, "Let him that is taught in the word communicate unto him that teacheth in all good things. Be not deceived; God is not mocked: for whatsoever a man soweth, that shall he also reap" (Gal. 6:6-7).

Chapter Six

The Lord's Teaching on Ministering to Your Pastor

Provide neither gold, nor silver, nor brass in your purses, nor scrip for your journey, neither two coats, neither shoes, nor yet staves: for the workman is worthy of his meat.

Matthew 10:9-10

"Take nothing on your journey: Give them the bill!"

Ministering to your pastor is a divine command. It is sad, but true that our stance on certain promises of the Word of God are dictated by "selective faith" as a result of selective hearing of the Word of God. This is the leading cause of denominationalism, and it is created when we take an unreasonable, immovable stand based on our own reasoning (or sometimes upon the indoctrination of the denomination we belong to or were raised in). Very few of us still have room for "the inspiration of the Almighty [which] giveth...understanding" (Job 32:8b).

The same Bible that tells us, "Ye must be born again" (see Jn. 3:3-7), also says, "Be ye holy; for I am holy" (1 Pet. 1:16b), and in another place also says, "Follow peace with

81

all men, and holiness, without which no man shall see the Lord" (Heb. 12:14). But how many of us are declaring "I am born again," and yet cannot equally say "I am holy." This, my friend, is the result of selective hearing and believing! We have cooked up every possible explanation against freedom from sin and being holy; but if it was impossible to be holy, why would the living God say, "Be ye holy"? As Charles Finney in his book *Revivals of Religion* puts it, "The plea of inability is the worst of excuses. It slanders God so, charging Him with infinite tyranny, in commanding men to do that which there's no power to do." If holiness is impossible, then from the above it follows that no man shall see God (see Mt. 5:8)! And if our hope in God is in this life only, then we are of all men most miserable (see 1 Cor. 15:19)!

The same God who "so loved the world, that He *gave* His only begotten Son, that whosoever believeth in Him should not perish, but have everlasting life" (Jn. 3:16), in turn said, "*Give*, and it shall be given unto you; good measure, pressed down, and shaken together, and running over, shall men give into your bosom" (Lk. 6:38a). And, of course, it is also recorded that our Lord Jesus said, "It is more blessed to give than to receive" (Acts 20:35b). However, our selective believing has rendered this aspect of worship ineffective. Worshiping through *giving*, or the time for offering, has become one of the least enthusiastic and least spiritual moments in the worship services in the Church. Contrary to Scripture, it is no longer time to bring the best of our harvest. Instead, it has become a time in church when we dig out our leftovers. It has become the time we bring the change out of our pockets.

To Aaron the Lord said, "All the best of the oil, and all the best of the wine, and of the wheat, the firstfruits of them which they shall offer unto the Lord, them have I given thee. And whatsoever is first ripe in the land, which they shall bring unto the Lord, shall be thine..." (Num. 18:12-13). However, this is not what we see during a typical worship service. *Giving* is not a capitalist word, and many of us in capitalist societies want to remove this word from our dictionaries. Pastor Jack Hayford beautifully states in his book *The Key to Everything*:

> "*Give* is a word that makes people want to run. Our fears have taught us that to give anything is to be left with less. But the best things in life come from giving:
>
> 1. You give when you learn to forgive.
> 2. You forgive when you know you've been forgiven.
> 3. You're forgiven because God gave.
>
> So the key to everything is giving.

Giving to your pastor is obedience to a biblical mandate. Yet because of our fears and disobedience in this area, it is rare to see the blessings from giving for the sake of the gospel flourishing in the Christian community. God chose to arrange things this way for our own good and benefit, yet we have refused to recognize and participate in His plan for us.

Yet the Lord clearly instructed His disciples, "Provide neither gold, nor silver, nor brass in your purses, nor scrip for your journey, neither two coats, neither shoes, nor yet staves: for the workman is worthy of his meat" (Mt. 10:9-10). This statement sends the disciple out empty-handed, almost naked, and 100 percent dependent on our giving.

Why is man, therefore, trying so hard to get around what has proceeded from the mouth of God? Could it be that

God's truth is too simple and basic? We know salvation is free, but many are paying to enter hell! The Lord said, *"Stand still*, and see the salvation of the Lord" (Ex. 14:13), but the Israelites (as well as ourselves) would have felt more secure having chariots and horses. We trust in material possessions and tremble in our insecurity, but the Lord says, "Go sell all you have, give it to the poor, and I will give you more!" He is saying to us, "Prove Me! Bring your tithes into the storehouse of the Lord and see if I will not open the windows of heaven to such a degree that you will not have room enough to hold it all" (see Mal. 3:10). But we decide to rob God. The Lord promises us that if we will only believe, we will see the glory of God (see Jn. 11:40), but we want to see *before* we believe.

Jesus' instructions to His followers in Matthew 10:9-10 were, "Take no money with you; they are to pay the bill." But we have selectively interpreted this to suit our beliefs. We don't look at the pastor in the same way as the disciples Jesus sent out. We either feel that our pastors are already receiving too much or that they are supposed to be poor and humble. We have decided to believe the myth that is propagated by our mass media as a result of a "little leaven" of a few fallen televangelists that pastors have and love money. But the reality is that pastors have very little money to love.

If we receive the above command as simply as it was given by the Lord and do what it says, there will be no need for committees and debates on our pastors' needs and salaries. The exodus of pastors from the ministry is largely a result of the church's failure in this area. A change of heart and attitude on our parts will not only bring an end to this exodus, but it will make the ministry of our pastors more effective. It is imperative that we receive pastors as was directed by the Lord who sent them out in order to better minister to them as the Lord requires of us. We must be able to see them coming and identify the ways in which they are empty-handed, as they were sent by the Lord. Then we must fulfill our responsibility to fill those hands. Consider your pastor or one who comes to your town to be empty-handed, with no money, no suit, no shirt, no pants, no shoes, no coat, no books, no toothbrush, no toothpaste, no home, no pencils, no pen, no tie, no food, no table, no chair, no bed, no blanket, no cup, no reading glasses, no computer, no bicycle, no water, no car, no broom, no gasoline, no pots and pans, no lamp, no pin, no scissors, no soap, no shampoo—and with absolutely nothing!

Empty-handed is how the Lord sent them out, and that is how we should view them and receive them. If the Lord sent them out with nothing, why should we judge them for what they have? It is none of our business! God sent them out empty-handed, but He never said, "Thou shall not receive." What a pastor may possess should never negate us from doing our part by giving to them. By the way, it is the Lord whom we should be looking and listening to, not what kind of car the pastor is driving, not what he already has, not what he has that we don't have, and not what he is already being paid. For how do you know if the car he is driving is a result of what someone blessed him with? How do you know whether the shirt he is wearing was given to him from someone under the inspiration of God? I stopped giving preachers my money or gifts; I give them to God. If we were to know how some pastors have acquired what they already have, we would be very overwhelmed.

Jesus has promised, "Lo, I am with you always" (Mt. 28:20) and that He will never forsake the righteous nor leave his seed begging bread (see Ps. 37:25). Many pastors can testify of the mighty works that God has done to sustain them! One pastor I know served in a church where the young people got together and bought a Jaguar for him. Someone who saw this could fall under a jealous spirit and say unspeakable things about him, yet unless we adopt an approach of seeing it from the Lord's perspective (i.e., each pastor has been sent to us empty-handed), many of our pastors will continue to suffer need and be victimized into fleeing the ministry. We are workers together with God. One will preach, another will teach, and the one who is taught will work to feed those who preached and taught, so that they can have more time to pray and study to teach more—and God will give the increase. (See First Corinthians 3:4-9.) This is the Lord's design, and it can be accomplished in no other way.

When Jesus sent out His disciples He did *not* say, "The committee that receiveth a prophet in the name of a prophet shall receive a prophet's reward." Neither did the Lord say that the committee that shall give a cup of cold water only in the name of a disciple shall in no wise lose their reward. The Lord spoke to "whosoever" of His children (see Mt. 10:42)! An individual effort is required, not a group effort. To be effective you must make it an individual, personal affair, an individual walk of faith, and do it as unto the Lord—a personal sacrifice to Him.

If the Lord sent the pastors out empty-handed, does that mean that they do not need the things they were forbidden to carry? Quite the contrary! The last part of verse ten declares: "For the workman is worthy of his meat" (Mt. 10:10b). God expects us to provide for the needs of those sent in His name.

Let him that is taught in the word communicate unto him that teacheth in all good things.

Galatians 6:6

Let the elders that rule well be counted worthy of double honour, especially they who labour in the word and doctrine. For the scripture saith, Thou shalt not muzzle the ox that treadeth out the corn. And, The labourer is worthy of his reward.

1 Timothy 5:17-18

In other words, the Lord is saying to the pastor, "Don't worry about this or that because the Church will supply all the things you will ever need. You are worthy of your service." Is the Lord counting on you in vain? Let's turn the tables around. Even though pastors are coming with:

**no money, no suit
no shirts, no shoes, no coat, no books,
no toothbrush, no toothpaste, no home,
no pencils, no pen, no tie, no food, no table, no chair,
no bed, no blanket, no cup, no reading glasses,
no broom, no computer, no bicycle,
no water, no car, no gas, no lamp, no pin,
and no tuition for his children,**

...the one being ministered to should supply all these things for him and his family—including that tuition and the payments for the phone, lights, gas, diapers, groceries, doctors, insurance, maternity experiences, and every other bill that may arise. This is what our Lord has instructed.

You need to take care of your pastor's needs from a heart of obedience to the Lord. Do it to the extent that it will even bring the fear of the Lord upon your pastor! Are you so foolish as to try to finish in the flesh what was begun in the Spirit (see Gal. 3:3)? I don't think so. You were saved by the preaching of the Word of faith, which is Spirit, so don't try to control your pastor with pen, paper, and committee policies and rulings. Don't try to control him by holding back your blessings of giving to him. Don't try to control him by shortchanging yourself by refusing to pay your tithes. No, continue in the Spirit what was begun in the Spirit. Pray for him. Minister to him to the best of your knowledge from the Word of God, and let the Lord do the purging in your pastor's heart by means of your example. Be that walking epistle that the Word talks about, and let your pastor read you and be edified. Minister until your only answer to his shortcomings is your ministry! Above all things and in all good things, in deed, and in prayer, having done all to humble yourself before all men and your pastor, humble yourself and minister to the servant of God that has been sent to you. By your ministry you may be able to rescue your pastor from being forced to leave the ministry or from the fires of meddling with the church's finances.

Compared to your pastor, earthly professions are making billions of dollars from a clientele less than half the size of the Body of Christ. The last time I took my mother-in-law to the doctor, I paid $179. She was in the doctor's office for about 17 minutes and came out with a Tylenol-3 prescription! There are even less fortunate people currently lying in graveyards that ended up there as a result of the mistakes of some of these doctors. Yet none of the doctor's time or expenses go unpaid for in spite of these mistakes! How many times have you ever read of a doctor admitting he made a mistake? Yet even if you don't pay his bills, your tax money pays for his efforts one way or another. That is why 13 percent of the U.S. Gross National Product is said to be spent on health alone! Yet your pastor, a worker "together with God," is far more than a doctor. Doesn't he deserve more?

The first consultation with my lawyer cost $100 upfront. Before I could walk out of his office not too long ago, I had to write a check for $231. My church has just finished paying the church lawyer $1380 for representing the church in a business transaction. He did not even have to say anything! He charges $80 an hour for anything he does for the church. Second only to the medical profession, law is one of the highest paying professions in the world. Yet your pastor, someone who works in the service of God Almighty and is a leader in the most essential system ever established by God that takes care of your soul, is the least rewarded.

Every time you see your pastor, know that he spent money to come minister to you. Ask yourself the question, "Did I spend money to have him see me today?" The pastor bought a soap, a comb, paid a water bill, an electric bill, bought some clothes, some shaving material, some gas, and a car, so that he could take a shower, comb his hair, wear clothing, and drive the car to come and minister to you. Did you play a part in providing any of these? Week after week, it costs your pastor money to stay where he is so that he may minister to you at any time, 24 hours a day, 7 days a week. Did you play a part providing those accommodations to him? Keep in mind that the Lord sent him out empty-handed. Not only that, but the pastor has a family that he or she must take care of who waits 24 hours a day, 7 days a week for him as he ministers to you. Did you spend any of your money, time, or resources to have the pastor and his family available to you, or has someone else done that for you? Remember, everything your pastor has or does cost money, but he was asked to take none with him. So the *only* way this will be paid for is through your sacrificial giving to the Lord!

Now if you have picked up this book today and you are reading it, I'm sure it is because you are interested in ministering to your pastor the best way you can. Let me assure you, this is pleasing to the Lord. It is the biblical thing to do. It is the will of our Lord Jesus Christ! Remember that He said, "I come and delight to do Thy will, My God" (see Ps. 40:7-8). He came to profit us with doctrine, reproof, correction, and instruction in righteousness "that the man of God may be perfect, thoroughly furnished unto *all* good works" (see 2 Tim. 3:16-17). I'll say it again: *The Lord's command left the **full** responsibility of **all the needs** your pastor should ever face in the hands of the local church—in your hands and in my hands. In the world it is said, "If the shoe fits, wear it." If you have been lagging behind in ministering to your pastor, then put on your shoes and let's go work together with God.*

It is time to take steps to fulfill and benefit from the Word of the Lord on this issue. It is time for us to become obedient and take action to:

1. Profit from this doctrine of the Word of God that has been long absent from our list of "important Bible truths";
2. Profit from this reproof from the Father, for the Lord is a consuming fire. God's wrath is reserved for the children of disobedience, and we don't want to fall under this group continuing to act in ways of which He has strongly disapproved;
3. Profit from the correction of the Word and begin ministering to your pastor immediately;
4. Profit from this instruction in righteousness from the Testament of our Lord Jesus Christ without which no man shall see God (see Heb. 12:14);
5. Repent and be not conformed again to the world from which you have been saved; rather allow yourself to be enlightened, reproved, corrected, and instructed;
6. Now "be ye transformed by the renewing of your mind, that ye may prove what is that good, and acceptable, and perfect, will of God" (Rom. 12:2b).

The issue is not what the pastor already has. The issue is what the Lord has said we should do. You will have an account or record to defend before God based on what you have done in reference to His Word. Your pastor has an equal obligation before God. You will be judged on what you have done. Three will be there to bear record: The Father, the Son, and the Holy Ghost (see 1 Jn. 5:7). The pastor will not be there to defend your record.

Every pastor called of God deserves our full cooperation and our fulfillment of our responsiblity for caring for him and his family. And the Lord meant for us to take care of *everything* with *no exception*! Our transgression in this area has sent many pastors to be dependent on welfare. And in countries where there is no established welfare system, pastors have either exited the ministry or live like beggars. This is not a good witness for the Lord. The pastors still fully deserve, "All the best of the oil, and all the best of the wine, and of the wheat, the firstfruits of...whatsoever is first ripe in the land..." (Num. 18:12-13).

Envious of Your Pastor?

At some point in 1992 my pastor, Benjamin Williams, suddenly showed up in church with some new shoes. They were not only slick, they were "cool." I mean, they were "baaaaad"! I really admired those shoes. And I don't think he would have had any problem with giving them to me if I had asked him for them. However, I found out from Sister Sharon, his wife, that his feet are one size smaller than mine. So I went shopping for shoes just like them.

Finding these shoes was not as easy as you might think, because some of the shops I went into did not even understand what I was trying to describe to them. My accent may have even confused them, but I did not give up my search. Instead, I enlisted some help. Now I'm sure you know that wives always love for their husbands to look good, so who do you think I picked to help me in my search? You are right. I recruited my wife Jeannette. And she was in agreement with me on this one. She knew those shoes would look good on me.

So one day we went shopping and actually found the shoes! I intended to take the shoes home even if it meant rushing to the bank before it closed. Moreover, the store had only one pair left, and the pair was *my* size. I even liked the color! While I was in that store I never put those shoes down for a second. I was afraid someone might snatch them.

Then it came time to pay for them, and the cashier asked me for over $200! I almost jumped out of my socks. I tried to ask him to clarify what he had said. I was certain I must have heard him wrong. Slowly he told me those shoes were "t-w-o h-u-n-d-r-e-d a-n-d t-e-n dollars," tax included. My reaction was very unlike his speech. Almost hysterically I replied, "They can't be." To which he responded, "Who says?" He didn't understand and by this point my mind had drifted away from him to judging my pastor.

How could he buy such expensive shoes? These pastors dress expensive! I left those shoes on the counter and went out of that place grumbling like a pig. My beloved pastor now was one of "those pastors." How could he wear shoes that expensive? Why was it bothering me? Few would admit this latent thought, but somewhere in my mind I became resentful because I was paying tithes and felt like he was living high off my money. (I hope Brother Williams still loves me after reading this!) And isn't it true that we often hold back from ministering because we feel that *they*, the pastors, already have enough of our money?

For a year and six months I lusted and complained in my heart about Pastor Williams' shoes. I even told Jeannette about how *expensive* those shoes were. Even though I never allowed my attitude to hold us back from taking any opportunity that arose to minister to him, that type of spirit should not have had a place in the heart of someone who wishes to minister to his pastor.

Well, a year passed, and while I was up in New Jersey one weekend a friend of mine took me shopping in a discount or consignment clothing store. And in that store I saw those shoes again! This time I maintained my cool. There was only one pair in the store and they were oversized! To show you how determined I was to get those shoes, I bought them and have been wearing them with a *double pair* of socks!

One month later, in the cold of the winter, my pastor's car would not start. I offered to give his family a ride to and from church. In the pastor's living room after church, my pastor noticed what I was wearing and said, "Those are some nice shoes you are wearing Brother Toby." To *show* how spending conscious I was, I said, "Yes, Pastor, I bought them for *just* $50 dollars." (That was in comparison to the real price [his price] for the shoes.)

Well, when the Holy Spirit does something, He does it good—right down to the bones! I can't improve upon David's statement in Psalm 51: "Purge me with hyssop, and I shall be clean: wash me, and I shall be whiter than snow. Make me to hear joy and gladness; that *the bones which Thou hast broken may rejoice*" (Psalm 51:7-8).

To my surprise Brother Williams asked me, "Is that how *expensive* those shoes are?" I answered, "Yes," but quickly added, "you did not know how much they were when *you* bought yours?" The pastor went on to tell me that one of the members had bought them for him. Was I shocked? Yes. *Mesmerized* is the word. The member had not just bought the shoes for the pastor, she also bought a tuxedo to go along with them. He never really knew how much they cost! If you follow this story well, you will know where I have fallen and realize how many of us fall and lose our blessings. You will see that it is not right to prejudge, sentence, or condemn our pastors for what they have and for being a beneficiary of the Lord's portion and sacrifice.

Satan's Ploy of Using Televangelists

...How beautiful are the feet of them that preach the gospel of peace, and bring glad tidings of good things!

Romans 10:15

The local church has refused to recognize that it is *the beautiful feet* of pastors *and the local Body of Christ* who see, hear, and bring glad tidings of good things to the *local* poor, sick, and homeless, *not televangelists*. TV screens don't have feet, and they don't bring glad tidings of good things to the shut-in. They can speak, but they cannot hear. Our *blind* TV screens display mega-evangelists to millions, but how many of these same evangelists actually see the misery around the local church community? These things are rarely witnessed by anyone other than the local church and pastor! But which one is well-financed? The mega-evangelist. Who finances the mega-televangelists? Local church members. Who is being forced out of the ministry for lack of support? The local pastor. Who suffers? The local community.

The silver tongues of radio and TV mega-evangelists can't see, feel, or hear the desperate cry of the poor, but they have successfully mounted a strategy to secure help from the local church member—much more than the local pastor and his leadership. But who is it who feels the pinch? Who is it who feeds and provides emergency aid to the local poor? It is the local pastors who, at one time or another, must provide some form of refuge and aid to these local poor. It is these pastors who see the despairing drug users, the sickly, the depressed, and the deprived. It is these pastors who have to talk to, encourage, and bring some hope to those who can't afford a television or a radio. It is the local pastor and local church who are held responsible by God for the evangelistic work in that community.

So before you send out your next dollar to a televangelist, think again, and make sure that your local obligations have been met first. TV ministries have their place in these last days, but never at the expense of the local pastor and gospel teacher. All the above place a burden beyond measure on the local pastor, and we are required to give the local pastor our best support by ''communicating with him in all good things'' (see Gal. 6:6).

Chapter Seven

Pastors on the Defensive

The central theme of this message is embodied by First Corinthians 9. In this chapter the Holy Spirit presents a monumental appeal for the support of pastors and gospel workers. The pastor's right to support from the church should never be an issue of debate or contention in the mind of the believer. The church is guilty of neglecting pastors and allowing pastoral support to become a devisive issue.

A respectable member of a church once quipped after I had preached on this subject: "I don't see why he is still preaching about that when we are already doing so much for the pastor." Unfortunately, she was taking a one-sided view of this issue. The heart of this message is not so much in the interest of the pastor as it is for the member! Let's stop "kicking against the pricks" and "hear what the Spirit is saying to the Church." This issue is as dear to God's own heart as our salvation, because salvation comes by hearing and hearing by the word of God (see Rom. 10:17). How can anyone hear without a preacher? You will never lose or go wrong by supporting your pastor and providing for his needs. To the contrary, you stand to benefit greatly. But if you withhold your support for your pastor because of some minor issue with him, you stand in even greater risk for judgment (even if you are 100 percent right). You cannot correct your pastor by going against God's commandment!

The Holy Spirit's appeal to us to minister to our pastors can be summarized in two parts. I will refer to them as *intrinsic appeal* and *material appeal*. Every Christian should read and reread First Corinthians 9 until he or she comes to *understand* how to minister to his or her pastor in these two areas. Let's examine the two areas together.

An Intrinsic Appeal

Speaking Evil of Dignities

> *Am I not an apostle? am I not free? have I not seen Jesus Christ our Lord? are not ye my work in the Lord? If I be not an apostle unto others, yet doubtless I am to you: for the seal of mine apostleship are ye in the Lord. Mine answer to them that do examine me is this.*
>
> 1 Corinthians 9:1-3

We have read First Corinthians 9 many times, and many times we have failed to recognize the seriousness and the dangers implied by this chapter to the unrestrained child of God. We must realize that this chapter came about as a result of some Corinthian saints *questioning their indebtedness to the welfare of Paul on the grounds that he was not really an apostle.* The charge of the authenticity of Paul's apostleship depicts both the church's rebellion against God's established authority and His command that "they which preach the gospel should live of the gospel." (1 Cor. 9:14). They did not feel any better about his needs than they did about his authority as an apostle. The charge seems to have been scandalous and made in the open like in the Church today: "He is not going to have my penny. I know an apostle when I see or hear one, and certainly he does not sound or look like one to me." These people refused their obligation to provide for Paul's needs. And in order to justify their error, they began to question Paul's authority and office as an apostle. Now, show me a church that supports its pastor spiritually, materially, and financially, and I will show you a church that loves and respects its pastor and divine authority. The reverse is also true in our modern, democratically-ruled local churches.

As in Corinth, the primary root of rebellion against the pastor's leadership can almost always be traced back to the unwillingness of the members to support the local pastor. This may be stimulated by a number of factors, including his effectiveness as pastor and often even a spirit of jealousy ushered in by the salary and benefits (if any) that are provided to the pastor.

Now concerning a pastor's effectiveness, let us not be ignorant. How often have we felt like leaving our church to go to another church where the pastor appears to be playing the shepherding role better than our own pastor? The grass always appears greener on the other side! How many times have we been critical of the pastor because he did not do things our way—he did not visit us when we were sick or he did not call when he did not see us in church? Sometimes we feel that the pastor's sermons are not "good" or "meaty" enough. We have been listening to some "Apollo" on radio or tape, and instead of using that to supplement what we are receiving from our own church, we use it as a standard against which to measure our own pastor's effectiveness. We forget that the Lord Himself said that His Word would not return to Him void (see Is. 55:11)—whether it's through Apollo or Paul.

With all these misgivings about our pastor, we grumble about his effectiveness and subsequently decide to take things into our own hands. We decide that the pastor will not be receiving tithes, offerings, or any gift from us. We declare to ourselves, "I know a pastor when I hear one. This is no real pastor, and he is not going to have my penny!" Who has bewitched you, my friend? Who told you that your tithes and offerings were being paid to the pastor? If you think that all your tithes, offerings, and gifts are a personal favor that you are doing for the pastor instead of giving to God, then, my friend, you are of all men "most miserable"!

Now regarding jealousy, how many times have we felt that the pastor receives too much money? As long as the pastor is being paid more money than what we earn in our own jobs, we conclude that he is receiving too much money. Paul was in Ephesus, and he was already receiving money from Thessalonica, yet he still expected those in Corinth to give him more. And how did they respond, "No way! Besides, Paul is not an apostle like Peter, James, and John down there in Jerusalem. And did he walk with the Lord? No, as a matter of fact he actually persecuted the Church as I understand it." We grow a knot in our stomach simply because part of the pastor's rent is being paid or because he is living in the parsonage and we can't understand why he needs any more of "this" or "that"! At every turn we try to grumble our way out of our responsibility of taking care of the pastor and his family. This breeds rebellion, disrespect, and a spiritually weak—if not dead—church. I know; I have felt some of the above. Even though I had done greater things to minister to my pastor, I let stupid $200 shoes hold me hostage to a spirit of criticism of my beloved pastor for almost two years! We urgently need to repent. Does your pastor feel like Paul did in this passage to the Corinthians?

We are fools for Christ's sake, but ye are wise in Christ; we are weak, but ye are strong; ye are honourable, but we are despised. Even unto this present hour we both hunger, and thirst, and are naked, and are buffeted, and have no certain dwellingplace; and labour, working with our own hands: being reviled, we bless; being persecuted, we suffer it: being defamed, we entreat: we are made as the filth of the world, and are the offscouring of all things unto this day. I write not these things to shame you, but as my beloved sons I warn you. For though ye have ten thousand instructors in Christ, yet have ye not many fathers: for in Christ Jesus I have begotten you through the gospel. Wherefore I beseech you, be ye followers of me.

1 Corinthians 4:10-16

Let's beware of our criticism of our pastors. No matter how justified we may feel, remember God's words, "Touch not Mine anointed, and do My prophets no harm" (Ps. 105:15). Vengeance is the Lord's, and He will repay (see Rom. 12:19). The emphasis used by the Lord in demonstrating His desire for us to support our pastors also translates into the fierceness of His wrath toward a pastor who is not producing fruit. Do your part and pray for your pastor, that God Almighty will help him do his part.

Beware of Dogs

Dearly beloved, in dealing with your pastor, be most careful that you don't fall under the heading of a "spiritual dog" because of your selfwill, disrespect, and contempt of his authority—especially through lifting your voice in disrespectful opposition to him. Is your pastor constantly looking over his shoulder because of what you may say or do next in regard to his decisions on certain matters, his sermon, the church books, etc.? Are you examining your pastor in the spirit that once prevailed among the Corinthians, which Paul addressed in First Corinthians 9? If you are, please spare him and his spouse the pressure! Apply some brakes to your attitudes and actions.

To ponder in your mind or to stand before your pastor and challenge his authority, his office, and his decisions is not only spiritual treason, it is one of the worst things you could do to yourself as a Christian. Ministering to your pastor, or supporting him, calls for a humbleness in spirit, obedience, and respect for the delegated authority set up by God. Many of us want the pastors in our churches to have their hands tied behind their backs with our own little personal programs. Then we make sure that any step a pastor may make away from our own opinions is met with resistance and stubbornness. This point cannot be stressed better than by referring to what the Bible says concerning this spirit of stubbornness and rebellion.

The whole Book of Jude, as well as Second Peter 2, speak expressly against this spirit of speaking evil against dignities and authorities. In First Corinthians 9, Paul is responding to those who spoke out against him, God's servant, and were despising his authority. Second Peter 2:10 claims that these people "...despise government. Presumptuous are they, selfwilled, [and] they are not afraid to speak evil of dignities." Summarizing statements at the end of Second Peter 2, the

Holy Ghost claims that these people are like *dogs*. Dogs are bold and arrogant. According to Norman Hillyer (the Bible commentator), "One who is bold is recklessly daring and rides roughshod over the rights, opinions, and interests of others—human or *divine*. One who is arrogant will not be deterred from doing exactly as he pleases by the challenge of any appeal to logic, common sense, responsibility, or feeling of decency" (Peabody, MA; Hendrickson Publishers, 1992, p. 196). One example is the boldness of Cain who was guilty of murder yet had the nerve to ask Almighty God, "Am I my brother's keeper?" (See Genesis 4:9.) Another example alluded to in Second Peter 2 is that of a dog returning to its own vomit (see 2 Pet. 2:22).

Please excuse my graphic language, but I want you to fully understand how horrible a thing this is in the spiritual realm. A dog has no decency regarding many things it does, including vomiting and defecating! It will do these things right in front of your yard—with no shame and no sense of decency. Even a cat is more decent and discrete; because after defecating, a cat will try to cover it up. The same cannot be said of dogs. Dogs do as it pleases anywhere, anytime, and with no shame or regard for who is watching. A dog is no respecter of persons, for it does not care where it is when it acts, even if it is on the White House lawn.

Do you consider yourself a spiritual dog? My friend, many of us Christians need to show the world some decency in our own speech. It is beyond my understanding how a spiritual leader can go on TV and radio and call the president, a senator, or some other representative names. That is arrogance, and it has no place in the life of a child of God. All power is of God. It would be better if we directly address our world leaders in writing or in person, if the audience is granted, to express our godly point of view instead of publicly showing arrogance and outright disrespect of established authority. This lose freedom of speech attitude has crept into the church and caused a great deal of harm in the Church of God. Have you walked up to your pastor, told him something "as it is," and still feel proud about it? May our Lord have mercy on us. Yet even Michael the angel when contending with the devil never brought against him a railing accusation (see Jude 1:9), and if an angel will not, how dare we? Now is the time to repent!

There are certain things that should only be done in secret. The intimacy between husband and wife is a good example. Of course the world with its inordinate desire and appetite for pornography thinks differently. But we are not of the world; neither are we suppose to conform to its ways. And there are just certain things that can only be done in secret. Very few people have ever seen a cat playing a mating game or become actually involved in mating. This cannot be said of dogs. Dogs will have no hestitation to come right in front of your house to mate. Even if they are disturbed or harassed by outside parties during the process, the dogs still won't part from one another until their appointed time.

There are some very serious spiritual parallels to this bold canine characteristic. Therefore any time you find yourself exhibiting or acquiring the boldness that will cause you to stand and talk without respect for God's established authority in the home, the government (society), or in the church, stop immediately and re-examine yourself. Whenever you find a child talking back with disregard to parental or elderly advice and authority, you can be sure that this child is heading for self-destruction. Whenever you see lawlessness and ungodly acts exhibited by an individual, beware of the consequences. In the very same way, when a member becomes bold and begins to question the authority of the Word, the preacher, and his advice, look out; for sooner or later, "the dog will return to its vomit"! The desire of an individual to come against the authority of the pastor is often so strong that there appears to be no deterrent! In some persons the desire to criticize is as strong as the instinct holding the dogs together in your front yard.

Just look around and you will see the manifestations of this "doggy boldness." You will see the boldness of homosexuals. You will see the boldness of kids killing kids. You will see the boldness of babies having babies of their own. You will see the boldness of the abortion movement and other ungodly political programs. Some of these organizations are the most well-financed because of their boldness. For example, homosexuality and the resulting AIDS epidemic are the most highly financed programs of any in medical research history. Why is this? It is because of the boldness of homosexuals! They have even begun their own Olympic games!

For these vile affection seekers, there is nothing harmful about having sex in the open. You will see them equally declare that there is nothing secret or harmful about men going with men and women going with women. Look at the wayward kids in our nation today. They are determined about what they want to do and what they believe are their rights. They are the most disrespectful set of people you could ever find. They have no respect for father, mother, the elderly, or even the police. And they die young to fulfill Scriptures. Dishonor your father and mother and your days shall be short (see Mt. 15:4; Eph. 6:2-3). This is the same spirit that causes our churches (as well as the church in Corinth) to despise the spiritual authority God has established.

Old Testament Relics

Being critical and rebellious against the office of the pastor or spiritual leaders is a common occurrence in God's local assemblies of all ages. The authority of divine leadership has been questioned and examined from the top to the grassroots ever since the garden of Eden. This type of rebellion is as familiar as the first-century church, yet it is as old as the Old Testament Pentateuch. At the rebellion of Korah and his company against Moses and Aaron, when Moses called them to come before him they replied,

> *...We will not come up* [how defiant!]*: Is it a small thing that thou hast brought us up out of a land that floweth with milk and honey, to kill us in the wilderness,* **except thou make thyself altogether a prince over us?**

> Numbers 16:12-13

Jude rebuked this same spirit and revealed that "these filthy dreamers defile the flesh, despise dominion, and speak evil of dignities" (Jude 1:8). Anyone who is willing to minister to his pastor must beware of the "gainsaying of Korah" (see Jude 1:11). The spirit of obedience and submission should play a primary role in our lives as Christians, and it should be the barometer by which we judge every decision before we take any action in the church or outside the church. By this principle we know, therefore, that we must humble ourselves and submit to the authority of the pastor. This will keep us out of any snare the devil may try to persuade us to

106

examine and criticize our pastors. The enemy is raging, and it is his duty to seek out ways to attack. And he always uses his best swing against the leadership of the church. Be mindful, and don't let him use you to do his dirty job!

It is a grievous and dangerous thing to make light of the unseen or of spiritual things. The Book of Jude points to the fact that Michael, an angel of the Lord, although he was fully aware that the devil was a fallen angel, never brought against him a railing accusation when in contention with him. Instead he said, "The Lord rebuke thee" (Jude 1:9). This was because Michael knew that before his fall, lucifer had been his senior in Heaven. He had led the angels in worship before the throne of God. David was also driven by this same passion and respect of God's established authority. That is why he dared not touch Saul, the Lord's anointed, even though it was pretty clear that the kingdom had been torn from Saul and given to him.

If God spared not the old world that remained rebellious but washed them away in a flood and spared Noah, a preacher of righteousness, and his household, what makes you think that He will spare you who is standing up against His established authority (see 2 Pet. 2:5)? If he spared not the Egyptians who would not obey the voice of Moses, the man of God, but fed them to the fish of the Red Sea, what makes you think He will spare you for standing up against his pastor? If he spared not Korah and his company who murmured against the man of God, but swallowed them up with a hungry earth, what makes you think He will spare you for standing up against His pastor? If he spared not the evil cities of Sodom and Gomorrah with their inordinate appetites, but spared righteous Lot, who was vexed by their filthy conversations, what gives you the impression that he will spare you with your filthy conversations against his dignities and pastors (see 2 Pet. 2:6-8)? Shall I fail to mention Balaam who ran after greed, Shemei against David, the Jewish youths who railed against Elisha's bald head, Ammorites against Samson, Hananiah against Jeremiah, Ahap against the prophet from Judah, the Persian jailer against Mordecai...? If God did not spare these, what makes you think that He will spare you for standing up against His authority?

Friend, you are standing on holy ground. Remove your filthy shoes of rebellion and stubbornness and stand humbly upon your bare feet and hear from your pastor what the Lord is saying. Keeping this in mind, "...Touch not Mine anointed, and do My prophets no harm" (Ps. 105:15). For vengeance is the Lord's, and He will repay (see Rom. 12:19). Let us beware, therefore, lest we fall into this same kind of error.

For if after they have escaped the pollutions of the world through the knowledge of the Lord and Saviour Jesus Christ, they are again entangled therein, and overcome, the latter end is worse with them than the beginning. For it had been better for them not to have known the way of righteousness, than, after they have known it, to turn from the holy commandment delivered unto them. But it is happened unto them according to the true proverb, The dog is turned to his own vomit again; and the sow that was washed to her wallowing in the mire.

2 Peter 2:20-22

You don't walk around speaking negatively about yourself because you love yourself. If you love your pastor, you will not go around talking about him or despising his authority. Because you love yourself, you seek to feed yourself when you are hungry. This is the same thing you should seek to do for your pastor, even if you feel that you are right and he is wrong. However you look at it, loving and ministering to your pastor is the only correct way to resolve any problem you might have with your pastor, because the Lord says we should love even our enemies and feed them when they are hungry (see Mt. 5:44; Rom. 12:20). In Hebrews we are instructed to follow peace with all men and holiness, "without which no man shall see the Lord" (Heb. 12:14). And by the way, the pastor is not the enemy; satan is. And satan uses whoever he can get to his own ends.

Even though the enemy will try to make us think that he is in control, we should always remember that God Almighty is the One in control of him. For He is the One who is "declaring the end from the beginning, and from ancient times the things that are not yet done, saying, My counsel shall stand and I will do all My pleasure" (Is. 46:10). This is demonstrated by the way the Holy Ghost used the criticism of Paul by the Corinthians to inspire a monumental defense for ministerial and financial support for pastors from the church.

Why did Paul find it necessary to begin each of his letters with a statement of his official position? Why did he always have to defend his apostleship in his epistles? The answer is probably found in one of only two letters in which he did not claim or defend his office as an apostle, his letter to the church at Philippi. This particular church was the only church that communicated with him concerning his need (see Phil. 4:15). This church was the only church that ministered to him with gifts out of respect for Paul, his ministry, and his apostleship. There was no need for him to defend his apostleship to the Philippians. They recognized his apostleship beyond a shadow of doubt. Their faith and actions were proof of his apostleship.

Paul found it necessary to assert to the Corinthians, "If I be not an apostle to others, yet doubtless I am to you: for the seal of mine apostleship are ye in the Lord" (1 Cor. 9:2). This lets me know that I have a part to play in making of my pastor a true man of God! On the other hand, Paul's letter to the Philippians was not from an apostle to church members who needed to listen and maybe repent. It was from a friend to friends who had mutual love and respect one for another. It was from a member of the Body to other members of the Body who were all working together with the Head, God. As a matter of fact, the Epistle was actually an affectionate "thank you" letter from Paul to his Philippian brethren. He was thanking them for ministering to him.

So maybe we should get over this critical spirit that we hold over our pastors for whatever reason. Perhaps it is time to replace it with a different spirit, like the one that dominated in the Philippian church, a humbling, loving, ministering (serving), and giving spirit.

Material Support for Your Pastor:

Have we not power to eat and to drink? Have we not power to lead about a sister, a wife, as well as other apostles, and as the brethren of the Lord, and Cephas? Or I only and Barnabas, have not we power to forbear working? Who goeth a warfare any time at his own charges? who planteth a vineyard, and eateth not of the fruit thereof? or who feedeth a flock, and eateth not of the milk of the flock? Say I these things as a man? or saith not the law the same also? For it is written in the law of Moses, Thou shalt not muzzle the mouth of the ox that treadeth out the corn. Doth God take care for oxen? Or saith He is altogether for our sakes? For our sakes, no doubt, this is written: that he that ploweth should plow in hope; and that he that thresheth in hope should be partaker of his hope. If we have sown unto you spiritual things, is it a great thing if we shall reap your carnal things?

1 Corinthians 9:4-11

Again, the central theme of the message in *Ministering to Your Pastor* is embodied in First Corinthians 9. Here the apostle Paul presents a monumental appeal for the support of pastors and gospel workers. His argument begins from the premise that he is an apostle and that the Corinthians are proof for his apostleship. Accordingly, he establishes and proves that it is his right (and that of any other minister of the gospel), to live from the gospel. Paul's final conclusion reflects the position of many suffering pastors today: As much as he has the right to live from the gospel, he has instead refrained from that right for the sake of the Church and the gospel.

A Defense by an Appeal of a Soldier's Rights:

"Who goeth a warfare any time at his own charges?" (1 Cor. 9:7a) A country's support of a soldier fighting for his country during and after a war is not a debatable issue in any of our earthly nations. If we are a chosen generation, a royal priesthood, *an holy nation*, and a peculiar people of God (see 1 Pet. 2:9-10), why should we not support our own soldiers? Why are we not supporting those who are at the frontline fighting for our holy nation?

111

The Commander-in-Chief of the United States, for example, does not spend a penny for himself in the course of his service and duties. Even his leisure trips are paid for by your tax money. From his shoe polish to the napkins he uses to wipe his nose and mouth, everything is paid for by your tax dollars. It appears the people in government have done a little bit more of their Bible study than we Christians. They saw God's design for caring for gospel workers, copied and applied it to their secular leaders, and have done a better job at it than the Body of Christ. We have robbed God! We have cheated and almost made a beggar out of the one who watches over our souls as one who must give an account (see Heb. 13:17). Even though our pastors shoulder a responsibility far greater than being the president of a nation, we have frustrated and chased them out of the ministry by greed and rebellion that would be unthinkable in the secular world. If it were not for the mercy of God, we would suffer the fate of Ananias and Sapphira; but the mercy seat shall not always be a mercy seat! It will soon become a judgment seat! *Understanding* is to depart from evil. So please, beloved, understand and seek the opportunity to minister to your pastor. The world provides for its leaders and soldiers; so as good soldiers of Jesus Christ who have been chosen by Him, let us minister to the soldiers of the Kingdom of God, acknowledging that we are not fighting against "flesh and blood, but against principalities, and powers...against spiritual wickedness in high places" (Eph. 6:12). One thing we can be sure of, the gates of hell shall not prevail against the Church of God (see Mt. 16:18)!

A Defense by an Appeal of a Farmer's Rights

"Who planteth a vineyard, and eateth not of the fruit thereof? (1 Cor. 9:7b) There is no farmer on earth who after toiling and tilling the ground will sow seeds without the hope of reaping the rewards of his efforts. His shelter depends on that seed. His food depends on it. His transportation, clothing, fuel, health care, support for his family, and every kind of need that may arise, all depends on that seed sown in the ground. So who plants a vineyard without benefiting from its fruit? The answer is *no one*. And which do you think is more important, the spiritual seeds planted by the ministry of the Word by the pastor or the carnal support the Lord requests you to give to your pastor? The Holy Ghost requires you to know that if your pastor sows unto you spiritual things, it is a just thing that he should reap your carnal fruits (see 1 Cor. 9:11). Don't you know that the carnal things that you give your pastor are made spiritual to your account in Heaven so long as you give it as unto the Lord (see Phil. 4:17)? What does the Holy Ghost say in Galatians?

*Let him that is taught in the word **communicate** unto him that teacheth in all good things. Be not deceived; God is not mocked: for whatsoever a man soweth, **that shall he also reap**. For he that soweth to his flesh shall of the flesh reap corruption; but he that soweth to the **Spirit shall of the Spirit reap life everlasting**. And let us not be weary in well doing: for in due season **we shall reap, if we faint not**. As we have therefore opportunity, let us do good unto all men, especially unto them who are of the **household of faith**.*

Galatians 6:6-10

When given in a spirit of worship and thanksgiving as unto the Lord, the carnal things that you give will go more

113

than 10,000 spiritual miles! That is why a cup of cold water given to a man of God in the name of a disciple will not go unrewarded. Paul speaking to the Philippians on the same subject said,

> *Notwithstanding ye have well done, that ye did **communicate** with my affliction. Now ye Philippians know also, that in the beginning of the gospel, when I departed from Macedonia, **no church communicated** with me as concerning **giving and receiving**, but ye only. For even in Thessalonica ye **sent once and again unto my necessity. Not because I desire a gift: but I desire fruit that may abound to your account.** But I have all, and abound: I am full, having received of Epaphroditus the things which were sent from you, **an odour of a sweet smell, a sacrifice acceptable, wellpleasing to God.***

Philippians 4:14-18

If you have been negligent in making your pastor a partaker of the fruits from the vineyard, start *ministering to your pastor* now. Ministering to your pastor, however, is not a passport to Heaven for eternal life. You must still be born again to enter the kingdom of Heaven. If you are not born again and give all you have to your pastor, it will avail to nothing!

Chapter Eight

"Give Me My Flowers While I Can Smell Them!"

In my early years as a Christian, I was away from my home and living in another country. One after the other, the pastors in my life literally stepped into the role of a father in my life. Without knowing the level of pressure that I was putting on them, I nudged them at every corner with every need and problem that came my way. And in every single situation, they did all they could to help me. These men did their best to fill the physical vacuum created by the large family I had left behind in Cameroon. They provided me with clothing that was appropriate for the seasons. In spite of their busy schedules, they took time out and went job hunting for me and with me.

One pastor and his spouse housed and fed me during a time that I could not afford room and board. One pastor supplemented my tuition once when I could not pay. Another worked out a way for me to travel halfway around the world to visit my family. Every one of them did more for me than I can ever fully express my gratitude for. These men of God recognized my sincere efforts to walk with the Lord in the new territory of my newly found faith. Even when I was insincere with the Lord and with myself, they did their best to bring me out of that condition.

These pastors provided me with the guidance and help that I needed to find my way until my road could become mapped out through experience and knowledge of the Word of God. They never stopped encouraging me. As spicy and aromatic as each temptation seemed, by God's grace their efforts stopped me from yielding and completely turning back to Egypt. They gave me their best, even if it was the last they had. I may never fully understand the level of sacrifice these men made for my soul, but one thing I do know: I am saved today because they never stopped ministering to me. They helped provide for me even though they had no secular jobs, and at that early age of my spiritual growth I could not have made it without their sacrificial support. I also know that I was only one of many newcomers in the faith who depended on their spiritual and material support.

With only a few exceptions, over the course of an entire year, Sister Weathers (a pastor's wife) fed 12 college students each week. We were from Japan, Cameroon, Nigeria, the Bahamas, South Carolina, Iowa, Florida, and Minnesota. She fed us lunch and dinner every Sunday without charge. She had three big sons of her own, in addition to Pastor Weathers to add to that number. I discovered later that they even lived in a farm house because they could not afford a home in the city! However, they sacrificed to purchase for all of us out of love for our souls!

Pastor Flowers

In 1984, I moved from Minnesota to Washington, D.C. In 1986 I met my third pastor in my life as a Christian. Our pastor had resigned, and our church entertained visiting pastors from other churches for several months. Finally, word came that we were going to have our own pastor. He would be moving to Washington, D.C. from Ohio to be our minister. For the sake of my example I will refer to him as F.C. Flowers, Ph.D.

Prior to coming to Washington, D.C., Brother Flowers had everything going for him. He was married and had two children. He had a successful law practice in Dayton, Ohio. His wife worked. They had a home, a couple of cars, and a wonderful fellowship with the Lord and the local body. However, because of their call to the gospel ministry, they left all these behind to come to Washington, D.C. They sold their home, moved to Washington, D.C., and purchased a new one.

I was not present for his first message to our church in Washington, D.C. But in describing it to me, my wife exclaimed in Cameroonian lingo: *"Da pastor na wa wa wa!"* That is to say, "The new pastor is a trip!" From that very first day, Brother Flowers was very inviting. He told the congregation, "For just a little while you will have to put up with my mess, and I will have to put up with yours. But the Lord has the worst part, He will have to put up with us both until we shape up or ship out."

As with all our former pastors, we loved Brother Flowers, but just like the other pastors, we fell very short in ministering to him as the Lord would have wanted us to. It did not take long before Brother Flowers found out that the income from the church could not support him and his family. As a result, he began to travel back and forth every single week to Ohio to work in an effort to support his family. This indeed took a toll on him and his family. In an effort to let his dwindling finances and need for family support known to the church in his own polite and humorous way, he started to interject his preaching with the phrase, "Give me my flowers while I can smell them. Don't wait until I die before you give me a truckload. I won't be able to smell them then." Strangely, this was said many times, on many Sundays over a long period of time; however, it continued to fall on deaf ears like mine. It was just another good message that we all enjoyed hearing, but few of us ever attempted to meditate or act on it.

It did not take long before things began to fall apart for Brother Flowers. The center just did not seem to be holding for him. His cars kept breaking down. I can't count how many times the church deacon (a motor mechanic) and others had to work on his car or pick him up from somewhere that his car had broken down. Soon he was almost without a car, then he lost his house and moved into a townhouse. Finally he and his family had to move into an apartment.

After one of those "Give Me My Flowers" messages, my wife and I caught on to its meaning and went home to pray. While at prayer, the Lord inspired us to take some money to Brother Flowers. We decided we were to take him $200. When I entered Brother Flowers' apartment with that money he was lying down on a couch. When I gave him the money, tears began to run down his cheeks. He thanked me in a soft, fainting voice. Brother Flowers sobbed like a baby until finally he was able to mutter, "Brother Awasum, thank you. Only the Lord knows what you have done—*only* the Lord. And He will reward you."

As we fellowshiped he kept saying, "When it rains, it pours, but I see the Lord is faithful." As I sat there watching him, I saw a man, so broken yet so believing, so starved yet so settled, so intelligent yet so humble, so poor, yet soaring high like Job in the midst of persecution. And as I reflect on it now, only the Lord knows what Brother Flowers' family, "our own pastor's family," went through without us knowing or even caring. Could your pastor be experiencing a similar situation? You would know if you cared for your pastor. You will know if you seek to *minister to your pastor*.

Well, two weeks later Brother Flowers died after serving our church for three years. When I think of him, the words of one of his favorite songs still ring in my ears: "Am bound for Mount Zion, way out in the hills, if anybody can make it, surely I can." He died at 35 years of age, leaving behind a wife, a daughter, and a son. He had no insurance plan, and he died leaving the family penniless. He left the family without a home, having lost their home in the process of pastoring! Even the cheapest insurance plan had evidently been too expensive for him.

Could it be your pastor needs to "smell his flowers" from you now? Before your pastor's condition gets any worse, why don't you stop right here and pray for your pastor. Ask the Lord Jesus Christ to reveal your pastor's need to you. Then ask for His grace to help you in providing for the need. As often as you do this you are ministering and encouraging your pastor in the work of the Lord. How much does your pastor mean to you? Have you told him that? May the Lord lead and guide you in this leap of faith.

The loss of Brother Flowers was very painful to me. I have already mentioned to you that I viewed my pastor like a father. It had a profound effect on me. Could I have done better? Of course I could have—if I had known then what I know now. God's people are being destroyed for lack of knowledge (see Hos. 4:6)!

Struggling in the Ministry Is Not an Isolated Case:

Weeks went by after Pastor Flowers' death, and the Lord kept dealing with me on the subject of "Ministering to My Pastor." The Lord helped me to see that Pastor Flowers' example was not an isolated case. I reflected on the pastors who had helped me along the way, and I realized for the first time that they had not helped me because they were rich. Very often they gave to me of the very last that they had because they loved and valued my soul. I also began to realize that many of our pastors have a lot of unscheduled responsibilities outside of the ordinary scheduled church duties. In addition, our pastors have many unplanned expenses added to their normal family pressures—many of which the ordinary church member will never be aware or be faced with. Again and again the simple facts indicated that pastors need to be ministered to by their congregations.

The norm has been to look to the pastor for encouragement and support. However, have we ever stopped to consider who it is that encourages the pastor? Have we ever stopped to ask ourselves who ministers to our pastors? Week after week we look to them for encouragement after encouragement, and counsel after counsel, but we have never considered ministering back to them in like manner! The children of Israel looked to Moses for encouragement, yet did anyone encourage Moses as they traveled out of Egypt? Moses was a man with emotions and struggles like we have.

He could have used some encouragement from the children of Israel!

Are not our pastors persons with like emotions and passions as we have? When the pastor is feeling down who does he call? When he is in need who does he call? Week after week he gives us dose after dose of his best in the midst of criticism. At times when he is led of the Holy Spirit to step on our toes to get us moving out of our little comfort zones, instead of repenting, we will walk out of the church halfway through the message declaring that the pastor has hurt our feelings. Some of us will run home just in time to make our conference calls and decide the fate of the pastor.

If we were in this thing as we are supposed to be—walking not after our feelings but after the Spirit (see Rom. 8:4-5)—we would have determined by now that the pastor is not the enemy! "For we wrestle not against flesh and blood, but against...the rulers of the darkness of this world, against spiritual wickedness in high places" (Eph. 6:12). And if we are to win against this kind of enemy, we will have to fight him on our knees because "the weapons of our warfare are not carnal [envy, strife, divisions, hatred], but mighty through God [through the disciplines of prayer and fastings, fellowship, and respect for authority] to the pulling down of strong holds...and every high thing that exalteth itself against the knowledge of God" (2 Cor. 10:4-5a). In effect, we should be happy if we have a pastor that hurts our feelings (our carnal mind) through the use of the Word.

At any rate, the departure of Brother Flowers made me determined that in light of the Word of God whenever God Almighty sent another pastor my way, I would minister to that pastor to the best of my ability.

Being a Pastor's Aid Booster (Armour Bearer):

The next pastor that God sent to our congregation made a number of church appointments, and as the Lord would have it, the pastor made me the "Pastor's Aid Booster." Boy, was I happy! Have you ever had a vision of what the Lord wants *you* to do and you decided it was for *everybody*? Perhaps when you became saved you felt that *everybody* had to get saved right away. At any rate, my responsibilities included creative programming of a special kind. Even though I had no job description, I created all kinds of ways to make the church *aware* of the needs of the pastor and the memberships' obligation to him and his family. One Sunday I bought 100 brown paper bags and distributed them throughout the church. Then I turned around and asked the church how much it would cost to buy lunch for the pastor, his wife, and their only child, a son. A large portion of the congregation said it would cost no less than $20. I then asked the church who would like to take the pastor out for lunch, and nearly everyone said they would. I told them that this was their chance to take the pastor and his family out for lunch by placing $20 in the brown paper bag. Before it was all over, we had collected close to $800 for the pastor.

During my first few months of boosting the pastor's offering, I must have looked and sounded like Jeremiah. It was as if I was wearing the yoke of the pastor's burden around my neck. I talked passionately about the subject without stopping, to the point of asking the church, "Don't you remember Brother Flowers and what he went through? That was like just yesterday! Have you already forgotten?" Those brethren must have thought, *Maybe Africans are very emotional people.*

I was agonizing over my past failures to minister to my pastor, and so I was just letting the church have it. If it had been possible for my wife to zip my mouth on this particular issue, she would have. We often fought about it on the way home from church. "Couldn't you put it another way?" she would appeal. "What was wrong with what I said?" I would reply. This went on for several months.

Finally a weekend came in which I had to travel to North Carolina. There was going to be another Pastor's Sunday that week, which meant that all the offering that Sunday would go directly to the pastor. Well, I knew I was supposed to be boosting it, and I did not want to miss it for anything. However, I knew I couldn't be there in person, so I wrote a booster's letter to the church. But when I gave my wife the letter to read it to the church in my absence, she read over it and then had the nerve to ask me to *rewrite* it! When I asked her why, she retorted, "The church is not your wife." That knocked some sense into me. From that day on, I learned how to better talk to both the church and to my wife! I also became more and more aware that my anxieties on this issue of ministering to the pastor were a result of inspiration from the Lord. I became more and more aware of the Lord's dealing with me on the matter. At first the response from boosting the pastor's offering was sparse, but it grew better and better with time. But could we even do better? The answer was definitely, "Yes."

In my efforts to discover what the Word of God had to say on this matter, I stumbled into one of the greatest treasures reserved by the God of the Word since the doctrine of tithing. The findings were startling to me. The more I dug in, the more overwhelmed I became about what the Lord had to say on the subject. I found that the Word had more to say specifically about giving to the man of God even than about giving or caring for one another in the faith. As a matter of fact, most of the verses that spoke of doing good to one another first began with doing good to a man of God. For example, in Galatians 6 the Lord first said, "Let him that is taught in the word communicate unto him that teacheth in all good things" (Gal. 6:6), before He ever told us,

And let us not be weary in well doing: for in due season we shall reap, if we faint not. As we have therefore opportunity, let us do good unto all men, especially unto them who are of the household of faith.
Galatians 6:9-10

Once again, the Lord did not have Paul say, "But my God shall supply all your need according to His riches in glory by Christ Jesus" (Phil. 4:19), except that he had already said, "But I have all, and abound: I am full, having received of Epaphroditus the things which were sent from you, an odour of a sweet smell, a sacrifice acceptable, wellpleasing to God" (Phil. 4:18).

As we have already noted, the Lord Himself declared that He who receives a prophet (pastor) in the name of a prophet shall receive a prophet's reward before stating that he who receives a righteous man (a member of the church body) in the name of a righteous man shall receive a righteous man's reward (see Mt. 10:41). In fact, the entire tenth chapter of the Gospel of Matthew is the Lord's instructions to His disciples regarding their work and how they would be taken care of. And the final verse of this chapter caps it all when the Lord says, "And whosoever shall give to drink unto one of these little ones a cup of cold water only in the name of a *disciple*, verily I say unto you, he shall in no wise lose his reward" (Mt. 10:42).

Furthermore, one of the 27 books of the New Testament, the Epistle to the Philippians, was written as a result of this truth. Complete chapters of the New Testament as well as numerous citations in other Scripture passages all stress the importance of ministering to your pastor. Until the Lord stirred this in my spirit and directed me to seek out His Word on ministering to my pastor, I had not believed or even considered the subject. My negligence wasn't even entirely my own fault, for ministers I had known had always preached about giving and caring for one another without once injecting God's specifics concerning caring for the man of God! Yet even these men had felt limited in their instruction because as men of God they naturally wanted to avoid being labeled as *money lovers,* even though they had no money to love. I am not a pastor, so I can freely teach about it and yet avoid this label. And to be doubly sure, when I teach on ministering to the pastor I don't take any offering lest someone say that I am begging money myself. Praise the Lord. Amen.

We Are Not Ignorant of His Devices:

This ploy to keep ministers from presenting God's truth on this subject comes straight from the devil. It is his design to rob the child of God of the benefits imbedded within the principle established by the Lord for those who care for His pastors. In every aspect where a child of God stands to be blessed, the devil will always try to intrude, to blur or blind the vision so as to steal the blessing. The list of areas in which the devil has tried to interfere and interrupt God's intended blessing includes divine healing, miracles, tithing, holiness, praying, fasting, lifting up the name of the Lord, the Holy Ghost, …and now *"ministering to your pastor"*. Praise God; we are not ignorant of his devices (see 2 Cor. 2:11)! God Almighty is helping us pull the covers off our treasure purchased by the blood of the Lamb. For those of us who will accept this truth of *ministering to your pastor* along with the whole gospel, life will never be the same.

How many of us have gone back the second, third, fourth time to a particular restaurant because we loved the food? Well, consider this: If you have prayed and fasted over a situation and later saw how the Lord worked it out and delivered you, you could only pray for God's mercy for anyone who did not believe in prayer and fasting. Moreover, if a similar situation was to arise in the life of friend, I am sure you would not just sit there! You would begin fasting again. If the Lord does a miraculous healing work in your body as He has in mine, you will undoubtedly pray for God's mercy upon anyone who does not believe in the healing power of the Lord, the God who heals *all* our diseases (see Ps. 103:3). The same is true of salvation and the unbelieving world, Holy Ghost baptism, tithing, and now *ministering to your pastor*. The proof is in the pudding. Don't just listen to the testimonies of those who have done it. Try it and you will have a personal testimony on record to use against the devil when he sneaks up at you.

Remember, the saints overcame him by the "blood of the Lamb and by the *word of their testimony*" (Rev. 12:11a). That is why the Queen of Sheba could not rest. She had heard all sorts of things about King Solomon, and one day she decided that she would go see them for herself. When she finally did, she was able to proclaim to the king,

...It was a true report which I heard in mine own land of thine acts, and of thy wisdom: howbeit I believed not their words, until I came, and mine eyes had seen it: and, behold, the one half of the greatness of thy wisdom was not told me: for thou exceedest the fame that I heard.

2 Chronicles 9:5-6

Therefore I beseech you by the mercies of God to not only take "trips" of discovery in prayer, fasting, and faith in God, but to also take a trip in *ministering to your pastor*.

Yes, just as there is overwhelming evidence in the Word of God that cites the benefits of prayer, fasting, and being born again, there are also even more startling facts extolling the benefits to be bestowed upon those who care for their pastors. The reward of caring for your pastor is so immense that the devil has fought with all his might to prevent this truth from assimilating into the Church of God. Come what may from the depth of hell, its gates shall not prevail against the Church of the living God.

Don't wait until it is too late to begin ministering to the pastor God has placed in your life. You may never fully know the blessing you will be to your pastor and his family. Your obedience may rescue them from unnecessary suffering or leaving the ministry. And God has guaranteed that you will reap the benefits of your ministry to His servants. It's time for the Church to understand God's economy of giving.

Chapter Nine

Spousal and Family Support

It is an unfortunate fact that most pastors don't own their own houses. They can't afford college for their children. And most pastors' spouses are living amidst the ruins of a failed dream for their families. They live under some of the lowest living conditions in our communities and suffer unfair expectations from an unsympathetic, unrealistic membership. Even though these spouses and children hunger for some of the same securities and nice things that many of us may take for granted, most of them have little hope or opportunity to taste of even the smallest of these blessings. If by God's grace they do, once again, they will risk the wrath and criticism of a jealous, accusatory church membership.

Despite the many sacrifices made by the spouses along with their husbands, the pastors' spouses have never been fully appreciated and therefore they have been often neglected and ministered to even less than their pastoral counterparts. To spouses of some pastors, life in the ministry has been one bad dream after the other. They have spent countless nights wondering how they can work in their limited capacity and still meet up with the demands placed on them unfairly by the local church membership. On top of all this, pastors' wives must often face raising their children virtually alone due to the weight of the demands placed on their husbands' time by the local church. This places an even greater strain on these women and on their marriages when their husbands must work additional secular jobs just to provide the barest minimum of the familys' needs.

We have watched our pastor's children grow up and acquire the spirit of Absalom. By our own actions, the images of the church community these children have received have been so negative that they don't want to have anything to do with church when they grow up. They have grown up to rebel against their father and the church. Daddy has not really spent enough time with them while they were still growing up. They also watched (and often experienced as well) the ills done to their parents by the church.

These children have experienced the poverty, the rejection, daddy's frequent tears of frustration, and the false accusations against their mom and dad. All these things have caused these young people to look upon the church as an enemy—not a refuge! They have experienced the pressures placed on them for being pastors' kids. They have been constantly expected to wear their father's shoes. And they have been expected to carry and fulfill a calling they've never even had the opportunity to hear or receive. All these things have helped pushed them off the wall and out of the Kingdom, yet we sit back and exclaim with wonder how that could have happened to a preacher's kid. The members of the Body of Christ are unwittingly playing the role of an accomplice to the devil in frustrating the Body of Christ and hindering the futures and callings of these precious young men and women.

In the spring of 1995, I was invited to give the Sunday morning message to a church outside Washington, D.C. The host pastor was not informed of the subject of the message before I spoke. When the service started, the pastor introduced me by saying that he would never give his Sunday morning pulpit to anyone he did not trust. (However, before the service was over, I wondered if this pastor could ever trust me with his Sunday morning pulpit again.) I took the pastor's remarks as a signal that I was welcomed and trusted in that church, so I relaxed and made myself more comfortable. The devotions went on according to program. Then I got up and preached! I preached on the subject of "Ministering to Your Pastor."

When I began to preach the pastor became visibly tense, restless, and shaken. It appeared that he could not wait for that message to end. As we have already noted, this is one message that pastors are not enthusiastic about preaching. The pastor was thinking, *The congregation will think that I brought this fellow to speak on my behalf.* There were very few "Amens" heard in that church that day—except for those coming from my wife and the pastor's wife.

After the message, the pastor rushed to the microphone to issue a public disclaimer, saying that he had not discussed with the evangelist (me) what subject was to be preached on, neither had it been his idea. He then proceeded to "defend" the church, as if in fear and in a manner that seemed to convey that this message had no place in that particular church. Calling the names of every member present, he passed through a litany of praises of how each brother and sister of that body was his friend and how helpful he or she had been to him. This may have been true, but I could hardly wait to get out of that church and run home! Unfortunately for me, my wife and I had accepted an offer to have lunch with the pastor and his family after the service.

We were all seated around the table, but before we had a chance to actually begin to enjoy the meal, the pastor's wife, who had worked so hard and had set the table beautifully, broke down and began to sob on my wife's shoulder. The pastor's wife told us in tears that flowed like running water how very unfair the church had been to them. She invited us to look at her. "Look at my feet," she mourned (they were very swollen). "My husband had a very good job," she sobbed, "with medical insurance coverage for all of us. But he left that job so we could come here and pastor. We interrupted our daughter's high school education by coming here. That caused her to miss out on a couple of scholarships to the universities." Many tears and intense words were forced through her trembling red face as she expressed the depths of her grief to us. I had never before seen this always smiling mother and sister in Christ in this light.

"Now we don't have the finances to send our daughter to school. She will have to work to pay her way through school. She should not have to go through this because we entered the ministry, for she deserved that scholarship just as much anyone else. But now someone else will receive it and she will have to work for her own tuition." In addition, this pastor's wife appeared to be very sick. Her feet were greatly swollen, and it was quite evident that her condition had reached such an advanced stage because there had been no money to initiate the treatment her body needed. Our pastors' families should not have to go through this kind of torment.

My food dried up on my plate and in my mouth. This had not been the first time we had experienced a disclaimer following this particular message. However, this had been the first time we had witnessed or saw anything this emotional and sad, especially after a verbal public objection to "Ministering to Your Pastor." I was unsure of whether to help my wife attend to this precious pastor's wife or keep attending to the food on my plate. My wife was more composed than I was. The pastor was visibly shaking like a leaf. And I must say that by this point I was comforted and a little pleased that I had preached that message. That message indeed had a place in that church.

Contrary to verbal opinion, that pastor and his family were hurting. Your pastor may be hurting too. Check it out and love them. Pray for them, send them a card, call them, send a good gift. You may be the Lord's hand today, sent to be "a very present help" in time of need. Your pastor may be running scared of you, but "love casteth out [all] fear" (1 Jn. 4:18). Be a friend and show it.

Shattered Dreams

As much as they would want to, a good many pastors have very little hope for their children to make it into institutions of higher learning. Once again, this is as a result of their meager level of income from the church. They have lost faith, hope, confidence, and trust in the church to help them through such family needs. The pastor's children used to be the most privileged in attending institutions of higher learning. Now they are the least privileged to receive that kind of education. Many preachers' children have grown up in such a state of deprivation that they have actually grown to rebel against anything that gives them the slightest recollections of church and the church family. We owe such sons and daughters and their parents thousands of apologies, and we need to repent from our actions. These children have sacrificed so much for a ministry to which they were never called.

The fundamental childhood dreams of pastors and their spouses (like owning their own homes, their own cars, their own bicycles, sending their children to college, etc.) have completely vanished into thin air. Since these couples entered the ministry their dreams have been replaced by despair. Their hopes have been dashed by our ungodly treatment of these brothers and sisters who "labor among us." Few pastors and far fewer of their spouses have a grain of self-esteem left in their bones. But in a true demonstration of godliness, these pastors and their families have "left all" and followed the Lord.

Some of these families have lost their homes, properties, and savings since entering the ministry. These have left house, brothers, sisters, father, mother, wife, children, and lands for the Lord's sake and "for His gospel's sake," but we have robbed them of the hundredfold reward promised them *in this life* by the Lord. We have generously dished out one persecution after another to them. We have consistently—from church after church and in worship service after worship service—given them a deaf ear, a blind eye, and a short hand to their ever-impending needs.

The Lord alone knows how many times some of His pastors and their children have had to go to sleep without knowing where their next day's meals would come from. Many pastors have had to preach on an empty stomach, yet these same pastors still had to spend their last penny to pay the phone bill so the church members could contact him whenever they needed! Some pastors have traveled hundreds of miles on foot to preach the gospel to dying souls. Others have had to spend every cent they had saved to feed or send home the guest evangelist of the revival organized for the local church because the offering collected was insufficient to cover the expenses incurred. Still others have given up every kind of convenience and luxury for themselves and their families to respond to the emergency needs of members, the homeless, the naked, the hungry, the husbandless, the fatherless, the motherless, and all the less privileged. I know a pastor who once had to surrender an entire paycheck from his secular job to meet a church emergency! This was not because the church was poor, but because the church lagged behind in supporting the pastor and God's work.

The list is endless, and it can include one emergency after another that pastors frequently have to deal with without the knowledge of their local membership. A good number of pastors could use at least an upgrade in their family's present living conditions. It is the church's full responsibility to minister to and support these families down to their very least need as commanded by the Lord.

If the church were to do what she has been commissioned to do, the exodus, the hardships, the burnout, the frustrations, the rebellion in children, and the marriage problems in pastors' families, in most cases would all be eliminated almost immediately. But the devil has cooked up every kind of lie to camouflage this truth in his attempt to hinder the servants of

God and the work of the ministry, as well as prevent God's children from appropriating the blessings they would receive for their obedience to God for giving. It is imperative that we get this truth into our hearts and make it flesh in our lives. Untold numbers of ministry families are awaiting our obedience to the purposes of God. It is very likely your pastor's family is one of them. We need to stop looking for where our responsibilities to our ministers and their families *end*. It is time for us to see where our responsibility *begins* and then follow through in obedience to God's command.

Chapter Ten

Supporting "Retired" Ministers

"The gifts and calling of God are without repentance" (Rom. 11:29). A minister's calling is a lifetime vocation. A minister's calling is not just a job; therefore, as long as he lives, even though he may cut down partially or completely (as he grows older) on ministering the Word, he will continue to maximize his ministry in the area of prayer.

The world would have us believe that a person's contribution ends at the age of 65, but Heaven knows that this is just the beginning! This is the time when the weapons of our warfare can be released at full capacity, and the flesh will not be in the way to carnalize it. It is as we begin to reach old age that we are finally learning how to fully live not by our own might or power but by the Spirit of God, yet it is at this stage that we begin to become despised by the people around us. When a minister reaches his maturing years the Lord says, "I can finally use him now to full effect," but we have been erroneously saying that this same person has become useless.

Now there are "ministers" who have approached their "calling" with a 9-to-5 attitude. These persons have considered the ministry to be merely a job. They have tended to limit their duties to eight-hour days and let answering machines take care of the rest. These men usually pack their bags for retirement as soon as they reach the secular retirement age. But these are not the ministers I am concerned about here. I am concerned about those true warriors of the gospel who fought the kingdom of darkness from the pulpit and are now fighting it in their prayer closet without a pulpit. We have despised and disposed of them. It's time we remembered that the "stone which was set at nought of you builders [has] become the head of the corner" (Acts 4:11).

If our treatment of these warriors has been as poor as we have described in this text, these same ministers are in for a far worse nightmare in their old age when they are without a pulpit. We must search out these saints and supply every item that these "now off the pulpit" pastors shall ever need. We need to keep them involved in fight against the enemy. They are our best warriors, and the Church cannot afford to go forward without them. We are doing many things in our churches today simply because we have the power and money to do them, not because God is in these programs or that He has necessarily even sanctioned them. However, if you involve an older, experienced minister in the ministry, he will be able to declare with confidence like Caleb:

Forty years old was I when...the servant of the Lord sent me...to espy the land; and I brought him word again as it was in mine heart. Nevertheless my brethren that went up with me made the heart of the people melt: but I wholly followed the Lord my God. ...and now, lo, I am this day fourscore and five years old. As yet I am as strong this day as I was in the day that

Moses sent me: as my strength was then, even so is my strength now, for war, both to go out, and to come in. Now therefore give me this mountain...if so be the Lord will be with me, then I shall be able to drive them out, as the Lord said.

Joshua 14:7-8,10-12

In the West, the traditional thing has been for these old ministers to be left out in the cold to fend for themselves. However they are the best and most experienced fighters we have in this war in which the weapons are not carnal (see 2 Cor. 10:4). Older ministers whose spouses have passed away are some of the poorest and loneliest people on the earth. Some have been locked away in nursing homes and forgotten. Men who have dedicated their entire lives to spreading the gospel and caring for the Body of Christ have been shut away and forgotten by the very people to whom they devoted their lives.

Imagine having spent your whole life caring for people and then suddenly being left alone. Fellowship has been your life. You were there for the weddings, the funerals, and the emergencies. You spent sleepless nights sitting with the church members with a sick child. Other nights you waited before the Lord interceding for the people, but now you've been shut in for three months and no one cares to stop by and fellowship with you, pray with you, update you, or share church's concerns about the community with you so that you can pray. You are considered useless by the world's standards and the Church has bought it. In effect, you are no longer considered to be a member of the Body of Christ.

If Jesus is the same yesterday, today, and for ever (see Heb. 13:8), why should these ministers be considered useless?

Why are they being ignored and eliminated from taking part in the Lord's work? Don't we neglect these saints who have given so much to us all their lives because of our greed and individualism? We don't want to be bothered by these old folks. They need too much care, and we don't believe we have the time to give them. We are too selfish to give away any of our money or time to minister to these old ministers. However, the Church has an obligation to take care of the poor and the old who could not otherwise take care of themselves. We are running away from our responsibilities. If we can seek these old ministers out and take care of them at our expense, I strongly believe that this will be not only pleasing to the Lord but it will be of the utmost benefit to the Church's mission here on earth.

And what of the spouses of "retired" ministers? These women have so much to offer in terms of wisdom and godly experience. These are women who have developed signficant strength in the area of prayer over the course of their lives and ministry to the church. These women have also often either raised or helped to raise many children in the church. Often these women have shouldered great responsibilities in the church and in the community. However now that the sunset of their lives have come, these women are also forgotten and neglected. Yet there is so much these women can offer to each of us and to our families in the church. We too can benefit from Paul's instructions to Titus:

That the aged men be sober, grave, temperate, sound in faith, in charity, in patience. The aged women likewise, that they be in behaviour as becometh holiness...teachers of good things; that they may teach the young women to be sober, to love their husbands, to love their children, to be discreet, chaste, keepers at home, good, obedient to their own husbands, that the word of God be not blasphemed. Young men likewise exhort to be sober minded. In all things shewing thyself a pattern of good works: in doctrine shewing uncorruptness, gravity, sincerity.

Titus 2:2-7

The Scriptures give many instructions regarding God's special concern for widows and the fatherless. Yet how often do we actually take these Scriptures to heart? When a minister dies his wife and children are often left penniless, homeless, and with few options available to them. We have often been guilty of failing to take care of these needs. How many pastors' widows have been forced to receive welfare assistance just to put food on the table for their children? How many children have been unable to fulfill their potential or their callings because when their minister-father died the sparse support the church provided was cut off and there was no money available for college or other training? Perhaps the family was forced to live with relatives just to have some type of roof over their heads. Is this the inheritance promised for the children of the righteous? Is this what God would have the families of His beloved servants experience?

As we have observed earlier in this book, many ministers find it impossible to afford even the most basic insurance policies. They have no cash reserves. Therefore, even the smallest medical problem can move the entire family into a state of medical crisis. In the case of a prolonged illness or a death, the whole family is thrust deeply into debt just from the medical costs or funeral expenses. Ministers often have no medical or life insurance, and the thought of a trust fund or account for their children's education is in most cases a mere dream.

Does our responsibility to a man of God and his family end when that man dies? I don't believe so. If we are responsible for the care of a minister and his family when that minister is at the height of his strength and service, how much more so are we responsible to care for that same family when that minister is no longer able to care and provide for his family! Often our ministers give us the chief portions of their lives, health, and strength. We have accepted their sacrifices without question, failing to recognize how little we have left for them to offer their families. Often the sacrifice of the pastor's spouse and children is far greater than we could know or realize. Yet these too are members of the Body of Christ, and their lack weakens the whole Body. Yet their strength brings strength and wholeness to the Body and glory to Christ, the Head of the Body.

Earlier in this book, I told the story of a pastor, "Brother Flowers," who died while in the service of God to our church. He and his family had given up a good home, community status, and a prosperous financial standing in order to come to Washington, D.C. and serve the Lord as ministers to our church. As a result of their ministry service, this family lost their home, all benefits, and even the presence of their father in the home as he sought to work a secular job and also continue in the ministry to which God had called him. When Brother Flowers died, there was nothing left to provide for the needs of his family.

The death of this man of God served as a powerful wake-up call to me regarding God's intention for His Body to care for those who minister His Word. God also began to stir the hearts of others in the church regarding their responsibility to God's ministers. Since that time a number of people have grown to understand God's heart and desire regarding ministering to His pastors and their families. And the Spirit has stirred the hearts of many regarding our responsibility to Brother Flowers' family. Individuals have stepped forward to help care for this family's needs, and we have taken the necessary steps to ensure that the cost of his children's education will be paid.

Many individuals are being blessed as a result of their obedience to God's Word on ministering to God's ministers. We have much yet to learn and so much more that we can do, yet God is honoring the hearts of those who are seeking to fulfill His Word to the best of their ability. What about you?

Is your pastor in danger of being forced out of the ministry in order to provide for his family? Does your pastor's family live with the insecurity of not knowing how all of their basic needs will be met? Is your church's relation to your pastor characterized by ignorance and neglect or loving care and concern? Is God being glorified by the witness of your care for your pastor and his family or are your actions and lack of care bringing shame to the name of Christ Jesus? Are you and those in your church missing out on the benefits and blessings of God by neglecting to minister to His servants?

God is merciful, yet He will count us responsible for our obedience to His written Word. In spite of what materialistic

Western individualism will try to tell you, you have nothing to lose by ministering to your pastor. The truth is that you have everything to gain in response to your obedience to God's purpose. Begin to pray and look for ways to begin ministering to your pastor today. Experience for yourself the mathematic principles of God's economy. Become God's agent of blessing to your pastor and His advocate for ministry to your pastor in your local church. If you do, I guarantee that God's Kingdom will grow and flourish in your area as never before and you too will soon have a testimony of God's blessing to those who care for His servants!

Chapter Eleven

Where Should I Start?

In conclusion, here is a sample list of things you can begin to do or rally the church to do to minister to your pastor. These are suggestions. You and your church should seek God's guidance for additional items appropriate for your pastor's particular needs.

Prayer:
Form a *routine* to pray for your pastor's ministry in the local church, especially that he many minister according to the will of God in Heaven. Pray that the pastor may daily present himself a living sacrifice, holy, acceptable unto God, and that he may be of good report and be filled with the Holy Ghost. Pray for his spiritual life, that he may remain up to date with his calling and with his relationship with the Holy Father. Pray that the pastor may be given to prayer and the study and ministry of the Word. Without the combined prayers of you and your pastor, all that may be happening in your local church—no matter how "exciting,"—may be mere works of the soul (i.e. *academic, intellectual, or musical exercises*) without spiritual significance. And without the

Spirit of life by Christ Jesus, members will unwittingly continue to be in bondage to sin and the devices of the devil.

A survey of pastors (*Pastors at Risk*, Wheaton, IL: Victor Books, 1993, p. 179) indicates that pastors spent an average of 22 minutes a day in prayer. This is very poor for anyone who should walk by the Spirit and not by flesh! Still an alarming number (57 percent) of those surveyed spent less than 20 minutes a day in prayer. For a pastor to spend less than 20 minutes a day in prayer is not only frightening but dangerous for the spiritual health of the church. Only 34 percent spent between 20 and 60 minutes a day in prayer. And as little as 9 percent spent an hour a day in prayer. It would be interesting to know how many of these pastors fasted once weekly, or monthly, and/or take two, three, or more days extended fasts! Once again, this is cause for you to free the pastor from any burden that will take him away from the ministry of the Word and from *prayer* and to become an advocate of this cause to your church.

Pray for your pastor's family. Pray that the sacrifices they make will not breed animosity or undermine family unity, love and respect. Don't make vague prayers; rather endeavor to ask the pastor and his spouse for specific areas in which they need prayer in and then pray accordingly.

Pension Plan and Other Necessary Peripheral Benefits:

If your church is not yet doing so, please research and establish a pension plan for your pastor's retirement. This *minimum retirement benefit* is very necessary but often ignored in a majority of churches. This benefit is a *safety net* and will prevent much of the hardship your pastors could experience when they retire from the pulpit. If the Lord does not come soon, this safety net will also come in handy for the pastor in moments of emergency and eliminate many of the worries of pastors and their families. Along with these, advocate that the church buys the following for your pastor, or at least consider funding of, a car, motorcycle, or bicycle; health and dental insurance; and a social security allowance (if these things are not already included in his/her income). Also consider purchasing a home for your pastor.

A Home

Remember the cry of Paul the apostle, "...for we are made a spectacle unto the world, and to angels, and to men. ... Even unto this present hour we both hunger, and thirst, and are naked, and are buffeted, and have no certain *dwelling place* (1 Cor. 4:9,11)." If your pastor does not have a home of his own, imagine what will happen to his family if he dies suddenly. Become a leading advocate for the building of a home for your pastor and his family even if he lives in a parsonage now. Parsonages are church properties and many pastors or their families are forced to leave the parsonage in cases of sudden death of the pastor or when the pastor retires. Usually they have no home of their own to return to. Let us follow the example of the Shunammite woman in Second Kings 4:10. To advocate and build a home for the man of God and his family is a very unselfish and godly thing to do; and it is pleasing to the Lord.

A Yearly Vacation

Given the choice, your pastor will take a vacation only *reluctantly*. Not given the choice, your pastor will *wish* he could take a vacation. With regard to vacations most pastors feel like a new mother (or father) leaving their newborn baby with a baby sitter for the first time. Although they will only be gone a relatively short period, they depart with very mixed feelings. This is evident in every heart that cares. Your pastor carries that same caring heart towards your church. Pastors feel that one little step away from the church might destabilize everything they have worked so hard to put together. The parents of that newborn always come back to pick up their baby with excitement. By the same measure, rally the church to finance a vacation and "force" your pastor to take it along with his spouse and family. He will always come back fresh, happy, and surprised to see that things did not fall apart. He needs a vacation because of his hard work in putting together all that he fears may destabilize. A vacation is not only good for him mentally, it is also healthy for his family. It also provides them with uninterrupted time and opportunity for the family to draw closer and heal wounds of months of "separation."

"Upgrade" Your Pastor

Your pastor must remain current in many areas. The computer is a very valuable tool in this modern era. Without a computer, the many valuable resources of the Internet will be inaccessible to the pastor. Bookkeeping will be tedious and clumsy. Communication and other things built into computer technology will be hampered. Your pastor needs a computer and training in computer education—word processing, spreadsheets, and accounting at the very least. Strive to buy him a computer and become registered in a computer training course.

Professional subscriptions to religious magazines, correspondence courses, and continuing education courses from seminaries and local colleges/universities are definitely a plus for your pastor. Convention workshops and seminars can also be very enriching for the pastor. Encourage and appreciate your pastor and his spouse with gift subscriptions to some of these items.

Update your pastor's attire with random acts of kindness. Communicate unto your pastor or his spouse "gifts with a meaning" for their ministry, for example a briefcase, a suit, a pair of shoes, furniture, or any other good thing you find that will bless them. "Let him that is taught in the word communicate unto him that teacheth in all good things" (Gal. 6:6).

Appreciate Your Pastor

When any of the above is done, we are showing our appreciation for our pastor. But your appreciation must not be limited to these things. If you appreciate your pastor, his family, and their ministry to you, let them know. And don't wait until you have something for them before you tell them. Encourage your pastor through phone calls and notes. Let him and his family know that you do appreciate them and their ministry to you. You will be surprised how far your words can carry them. Please don't flatter anyone, but simply say what's in your heart. Have freedom, give generously, and let the inspiration of the Almighty guide you into other areas where He would have you minister to the pastor He has placed over you.

Evangelize!

Show me an evangelistic/mission-minded person, and I will show you a person who appreciates his/her pastor's ministry. Many believers in North America are fascinated with the number of people turning to the Lord in Africa, South

America, Asia, and the former Eastern block. What they fail to see is the fact that the inflow in these areas is not caused by pastors or evangelists but by the members of the local church through personal evangelism. Millions of persons in Africa, like myself, become believers through the witness of members of the local church. Become a self-appointed member of the local church's evangelistic team and become involved in bringing others to the Lord. After they have come to the Lord, teach them the *value, benefits*, and *responsibility* of ministering and supporting the pastor. When it is learned early in the faith, it becomes part of the lifestyle of the Christian. My beloved brethren, in double honor, minister, minister, and minister to your pastor. Be steadfast, unmoveable, always abounding in the work of the Lord, for you know that your labor in the Lord will *not* be in vain (see 1 Cor. 15:58).

For additional information or to schedule the author to speak to your church, please write to him in care of:

The Gospel Workers' Support Fund
P.O. Box 88
Germantown, MD 20875

Other
Destiny Image titles
you will enjoy reading

PREACHERS ARE PEOPLE TOO!
by Dr. Gerald G. Loyd.
We in the Church need to learn to balance God's demand for righteousness with His demand for mercy and grace. Preachers often don't have anyone to turn to when they have problems. *Preachers Are People Too!* is for all who seek to understand hurting leaders.
Paperback Book, 266p. ISBN 1-56043-817-7 Retail $9.99

IT'S THE WALK NOT THE TALK
by LaFayette Scales.
Lots of people talk about spiritual growth, but how many really demonstrate it? This book outlines and describes six levels of spiritual maturity and shows you how to move up to the higher levels of God's purpose for His children. Start traveling the path to spiritual maturity in Christ because, after all, it's the walk, not the talk, that counts!
Paperback Book, 196p. ISBN 1-56043-170-9 Retail $9.99

GROWING IN CHRISTIAN MATURITY
by Herman Riffel.
Author Herman Riffel illustrates the power of inner healing and the great release that comes to troubled souls, and touches on the many ways God speaks to us. This book shows what tremendous power has been given God's sons and daughters and describes the true manifestations of His gifts to us. Discover what God can do through and for humanity! (Previously published as *Christian Maturity.*)
Paperback Book, 210p. ISBN 1-56043-191-1 Retail $9.99

Available at your local Christian bookstore.

nternet: http://www.reapernet.com

Prices subject to change without notice.

Exciting titles by T.D. Jakes

CAN YOU STAND TO BE BLESSED?

You ask God to bless you and difficulties arise. Why? This book will release the hidden strength within you to go on in God, fulfilling the destiny He has for you. The way to this success is full of twists and turns, yet you can make it through to incredible blessing in your life. The only question left will be, *Can You Stand to Be Blessed?*

Paperback Book, 196p. ISBN 1-56043-801-0 Retail $9.99

CAN YOU STAND TO BE BLESSED? WORKBOOK

Paperback Book, 48p. ISBN 1-56043-812-6 (8½" X 11") Retail $7.99

NAKED AND NOT ASHAMED

With a powerful anointing, Bishop T.D. Jakes challenges us to go below the surface and become completely and honestly vulnerable before God and man. In relationships, in prayer, in ministry—we need to be willing to be open and transparent. Why do we fear? God already knows us, but He cannot heal our hidden hurts unless we expose them to Him. Only then can we be *Naked and Not Ashamed*!

Paperback Book, 156p. ISBN 1-56043-835-5 (6" X 9") Retail $9.99

NAKED AND NOT ASHAMED WORKBOOK

Paperback Book, 56p. ISBN 1-56043-259-4 (8½" X 11") Retail $7.99

WOMAN, THOU ART LOOSED!

This book offers healing to hurting single mothers, insecure women, and battered wives; and hope to abused girls and women in crisis! Hurting women around the nation—and those who minister to them—are devouring the compassionate truths in Bishop T.D. Jakes' *Woman, Thou Art Loosed!*

Paperback Book, 210p. ISBN 1-56043-100-8 Retail $9.99

WOMAN, THOU ART LOOSED! WORKBOOK

Paperback Book, 48p. ISBN 1-56043-810-X (8½" X 11") Retail $7.99

Exciting titles
by Dr. Wanda Davis-Turner

Other *Destiny Image titles* you will enjoy reading

DON'T DIE IN THE WINTER...
by Dr. Millicent Thompson.

Why do we go through hard times? Why must we suffer pain? In *Don't Die in the Winter...* Dr. Thompson explains the spiritual seasons and cycles that people experience. A spiritual winter is simply a season that tests our growth. We need to endure our winters, for in the plan of God, spring always follows winter!
Paperback Book, 168p. ISBN 1-56043-558-5 Retail $8.99

CRASHING SATAN'S PARTY
by Dr. Millicent Thompson.

Don't let satan hinder the power of God from working in your life any longer! In this book you'll discover the strategies and devices the enemy uses against you. Too many of us attribute our troubles to God when they are really of the devil. The adversary is subtle and delights in deception. We must be able to recognize *who* is doing *what* in our lives so that we can react according to God's Word. Learn how to destroy the works of the enemy. You can crash satan's party and overcome!
Paperback Book, 144p. ISBN 1-56043-268-3 (6" X 9") Retail $10.99

HOW TO RAISE CHILDREN OF DESTINY
by Dr. Patricia Morgan.

This groundbreaking book highlights the intricate link between the rise of young prophets, priests, and kings in the Body of Christ as national leaders and deliverers, and the salvation of a generation
Paperback Book, 210p. ISBN 1-56043-134-2 Retail $9.99

THE BATTLE FOR THE SEED
by Dr. Patricia Morgan.

The dilemma facing young people today is a major concern for all parents. This important book of the 90's shows God's way to change the condition of the young and advance God's purpose for every nation into the next century.
Paperback Book, 112p. ISBN 1-56043-099-0 Retail $9.99

Available at your local Christian bookstore.

nternet: http://www.reapernet.com

Prices subject to change without notice.